C000300440

NEIL FINDLAY left school at 16 and wor
bricklayer along with his father. WI
classes at college before going to univ
as a housing officer and school teache
strike and the poll tax and joined the Labour Party at 18. In 2003 he
was elected onto West Lothian Council and from 2011–21 he was an
MSP in the Scottish Parliament. He is a campaigner, a socialist and a
trade unionist. He lives in the mining community of Fauldhouse in West
Lothian and is married to Fiona. They have one daughter, Chloe.

By the same author:

Socialism & Hope, Luath Press, 2017
Life in the Raws (with Jock Findlay), Luath Press, 2020

If You Don't Run, They Can't Chase You

NEIL FINDLAY

Luath Press Limited
EDINBURGH
www.luath.co.uk

First published 2021

ISBN: 978-1-910022-43-6

The author's right to be identified as author of this book
under the Copyright, Designs and Patents Act 1988 has been asserted.

The paper used in this book is recyclable. It is made
from low chlorine pulps produced in a low energy,
low emission manner from renewable forests.

Printed and bound by
Severn, Gloucester

Typeset in 11 point Sabon by
Main Point Books, Edinburgh

P.33 Photograph of Terry Renshaw reproduced with the kind permission of Media Wales.
P.42 Photograph of Brian Filling with Nelson Mandela reproduced with the kind
permission of the photographer, Alan Wylie.
P.57 Photograph of Maria Fyfe reproduced with the kind permission of the
photographer, Stephen Fyfe.
P.122 Photograph of Margaret Aspinall by Geoff Davies reproduced with the kind
permission of Geoff Davies/*The Liverpool Echo.*
All other images © Neil Findlay or the subject.

Dedicated to social justice campaigners across the world

Contents

Note

THE TITLE OF this books comes from a quote by Michael McGahey, former Vice President of the National Union of Mineworkers. He used it during the miners' strike of 1984–85, urging his comrades to stand up to the actions of their employer, the government and the state machinery that was being used against them. It exemplifies the spirit of the people I feature in these pages: none of them ran.

Note

Introduction

THE FINANCIAL CRASH of 2008 shook the world. The seemingly unstoppable march of global capitalism was hit by an earthquake and some of the biggest names in the world of finance were exposed as cheats, liars and fraudsters. Previously respected members of the financial establishment like Lehman Brothers, the Royal Bank of Scotland and Fannie Mae and Freddy Mac were joined by household names like Tesco, Amazon and Starbucks in an exposure of the workings of the 'free market'.

The public were rightly furious that systemic corruption and corporate greed, in the shape of industrial-scale tax avoidance, the mis-selling of financial products, dodgy accountancy practices and repeated customer rip-offs, were commonplace. People were outraged that senior executives in corporations which had been involved in these practices for decades retained their telephone number salaries and huge bonuses. Meanwhile, back in the real world, their customers lost their jobs, homes, pensions, businesses and savings. Workers around the world experienced wage cuts and stagnation, unemployment increased, food bank use soared, and exploitative working practices and job insecurity became the norm in many sectors.

Thatcherite economics was re-branded as 'austerity' and rolled out across the European Union, where Ireland and Greece had their democratically elected governments' budgets rewritten by the International Monetary Fund (IMF), the European Central Bank (ECB) and the European Commission – the so-called 'Troika' – without a single vote ever having been cast for any of these mysterious but all-powerful men and women.

Youth unemployment hit 50 per cent in Greece and 40 per cent in Spain, and in 22 countries across the EU reached over 20 per cent. Pensions were cut, poverty and malnutrition increased, and rickets returned. Public services were sold off or decimated by privatisation and cuts.

In such circumstances, the left should have come to the fore to lead a global movement pinning the blame firmly on those who were at fault – the speculators, the free marketeers, the hedge fund managers and corporate tax avoiders. The left should have offered a radical, sustainable, progressive alternative agenda. But that never happened.

Early glimmers of hope in the shape of the 'We are the 99%' movement soon fizzled out and it was the forces of the right who filled the gap, most nauseatingly exemplified by the grotesque figure of Trump in the US, but also by Cameron and Osborne in the UK, Bolsonaro in Brazil, 'The League' in Italy and Orbán in Hungary. Across Europe, far-right, anti-immigration political parties made significant gains. Extreme nationalism became the go-to destination for many of those seeking answers. Only in Portugal and Spain did parties of the left win power.

In the UK, the Labour Party, under the leadership of Jeremy Corbyn, was predicted to go down in a humiliating defeat at the 2017 election, but it didn't quite turn out like that. Corbyn prevented a Tory majority – standing on a socialist programme, not quite *The Communist Manifesto* but certainly more radical than anything Labour had offered in decades.

Spooked by the possibility of a Labour victory in 2019 and with another election imminent, the dogs of war were unleashed on Corbyn, John McDonnell and anyone associated with them. Day in, day out, the media, from *The Sun* and *Daily Mail*, to *Sky News*, the BBC, social media commentators, TV personalities, pundits and a number of Corbyn's fellow Labour MPs, including within his Shadow Cabinet, joined the feeding frenzy. Every issue, big or small, became weaponised and used to attack him and his policy agenda. A man who had been involved in the peace movement all his life was portrayed as a terrorist sympathiser. A consistent campaigner for minority rights, refugees and those affected by war and conflict, Corbyn was portrayed as an anti-Semite and a racist. The writings and actions of Boris Johnson, or of the architect of 'the hostile environment' against immigrants, Theresa May, were ignored. Such was the level and absurdity of these attacks on Corbyn that even his bike was fair game – a *Times* journalist referring to it as a 'Chairman Mao-style bicycle'– WTF? *Newsnight* joined in by photoshopping an image of Corbyn in a 'Lenin cap' against a backdrop of the Kremlin to portray him as a friend of the Russians. These attacks were cheered on, endorsed and fed by certain Labour MPs, including Ian Austin, Chris Leslie, Ian Murray, Mike Gapes and Jess Phillips. It has since transpired that an ultra-right-wing section of the party bureaucracy worked diligently to undermine the efforts of members and candidates who were not in their faction. Anyone to the left of Gordon Brown was deemed 'a Trot'. These same critics were then apparently astonished that their daily attacks on their own side had a very real impact, culminating in the disaster of the December 2019 General Election result.

At the mercy of the right-wingers in Northern Ireland's DUP and the equally right-wing Tory Brexiteers, Theresa May – unable to placate these factions and deliver her Brexit deal – had been toppled by the populist, establishment figure of Boris Johnson, who then cast aside Tory divisions and exploited Labour's internal warfare and lack of unity to win a landslide election victory. A view widely touted by the media, that if only Labour had got rid of Corbyn then they would have been 20 points ahead in the polls against a poor Prime Minister (May) and a hopeless Prime Minister (Johnson), has been shown up as nonsense, as the current Labour leader, Sir Keir Starmer, trails Johnson miserably in polls.

It would be easy to despair at this state of play, but we must not; indeed, we cannot. Instead, the left must learn the lessons from our past and draw inspiration from those who have gone before us. We must examine the campaigns and struggles people have gone through, listen to their stories, study their actions and in turn look at the world now, and apply what we have learned to build new movements to campaign and deliver the changes we want to see.

We know that those who hold power never give up willingly; change only comes through determined action, by taking a stand, often initially unpopular, before the demands are popularised through various actions. This often requires trailblazers who are willing to take risks and make issues 'safe' for others to join in, build momentum and turn demands into real change.

Actions can be defensive, to retain what we already have; or offensive, to demand that something is done differently. This book was written to show how key struggles and campaigns have emerged over the last 50 years or so to challenge the status quo, make demands of those in power, and often against the greatest of odds, bring about major social and economic change.

These struggles and campaigns were tough, brutal and always life-changing for those involved. They required bravery, leadership, personal sacrifice, tenacity, organisation, skill and drive to see them through to their conclusion.

Some resulted in glorious victory, others in crushing defeat, but all of them teach us something about the human spirit, about promoting and defending ideals and principles, about personal strength, collective action, leadership, justice, democracy and common decency.

Young activists of today, social justice campaigners, trade unionists, environmentalists, politicians and those who have found a new zest for activism in their later years will find these accounts inspirational, emotional and, I hope, educational.

The people I have interviewed have been chosen for a variety of reasons. Some, like Alistair Mackie and Jim Swan, are people I have known for decades and who were mentors to me as a young political activist. Others, like Dennis Skinner and the late Maria Fyfe, are public figures I admire: campaigners and activists first, parliamentarians second.

Mark Lyon, 'Andrea', Dave Smith, Terry Renshaw and Tony Nelson are trade unionists whose commitment, determination and drive for social justice has left a huge impression on me. They are shining examples of what can happen when working people organise and refuse to be browbeaten by powerful forces, no matter the odds stacked against them.

And in Brian Filling, Louise Adamson, Margaret Aspinall, Elaine Holmes and Olive McIlroy, I see the very best of humanity: people from ordinary backgrounds achieving extraordinary things, not for fame or fortune, self-promotion or self-interest, but for the good of other people, for the good of their community, or for the good of those they have never or may never meet. (Please be aware that in transcribing my interviews with them, I have favoured the styles and cadences of the spoken word over 'standard English'.)

Let us be driven by their stories to make the world a better place by building a future on the foundations of the enduring values of fairness, dignity, equality, justice, co-operation and solidarity. As the COVID-19 crisis has shown, it is these values, the values of socialism, that we turn to in our time of need.

Neil Findlay,
Fauldhouse, July 2021

What Makes a Good Campaign?

THIS BOOK FEATURES INTERVIEWS with and testimonies from people, some of whom I have campaigned alongside and others who have inspired and motivated me from afar. Their commitment, determination and innovative approach to the causes they hold dear is inspirational.

Many individuals take up issues and establish campaigns because no one else will. The establishment can often look on campaigners as obsessive cranks to be easily silenced and dismissed, or at best kept at arm's length, ignored, written off or mocked. They may already have approached organisations such as political parties, charities, trade unions or NGOs for help and been rebuffed entirely or met with ambivalence, indifference, 'small c' conservatism, or a complete misunderstanding of the issues they raise. Of course, these organisations have their own pressures and there can be entirely legitimate reasons for their lack of support or engagement. It may be a lack of knowledge, personnel or financial resources, or they may come under pressure from funders if they take up causes that upset their paymasters such as central or local government, other NGOs or corporate funders. New campaigns can seriously challenge some of the most respected and well-known third sector organisations – they are often seen as a rebellious irritant to be ignored in the hope they will go away and 'let the big sensible boys and girls get on with the job'. But steady-as-you-go, patient, polite gradualism can suffocate enthusiasm and suck the life and energy out of the motivated and those driven by the key ingredient of any campaign: PASSION.

The chapters of this book allow some of the most passionate campaigners you will find anywhere to explain in their own words what has driven their campaign. Most never sought the limelight, they were thrust into campaigns because of circumstances or events outside their control and because the actions of others affected their lives, all too often in a negative way. They decided enough was enough and made the decision to act. From small, tentative steps,

action commitment
communications
ideas determination media
objectives organisation passion
people teamwork

buoyed by the force of their argument and belief in the issue at stake and a sense of injustice, these people and their campaigns emerged into the public domain. Campaigns can begin with one key ask or aim but over time – as new events happen or information is unearthed, leaked or published – the campaign can change direction. Success or failure is often determined by how clear, understandable and easily communicated objectives are. The importance of this cannot be overestimated. Everyone knows that the red ribbon is the symbol of HIV solidarity or the colour pink is associated with breast cancer.

While being driven by injustice and having a clear message is of critical importance, campaigns need people. Campaigns have to be led, they need planning and they need skilled activists to help execute them. They don't just happen.

Mass campaigns often grow from humble beginnings. Who would have thought that the determined, solitary actions of a young Swedish schoolgirl, Greta Thunberg, could have resulted in the global school strike phenomenon?

As campaigns grow and develop they need people to take on tasks: research, organising activists, media work (including social media), lobbying those in power, fundraising... there are always things to do.

Some of the campaigns featured in this book came before the emergence of mobile phones, 24-hour news coverage, the internet and social media. Easy, quick access to information via the internet and mobile phones has had a phenomenal impact on campaigns, raising awareness of issues, allowing information to be shared immediately, organising actions and helping raise funds. It is in this area of digital campaigning where real creative innovation has grabbed the attention of the public and taken campaigns to a global audience. 'The ice bucket challenge' videos raised over $100 million in the US alone for research into Motor Neurone Disease and other neurological conditions, with a global audience sharing videos of people having buckets of cold water poured over their heads. This simple idea made a huge global impact, communicating a serious message in a fun way and raising a huge amount of money in the process.

The creative use of video, graphics, Facebook ads, Twitter storms, YouTube videos, Instagram and so on creates a reach that no one could ever have imagined 20 years ago. Campaigns, ideas and messages can reach mass audiences at the click of a mouse, building communities of interest and coalitions of support from near and far. These are just some of the main ingredients for a successful campaign – you will be able to identify them throughout the chapters of this book. I hope they will help you develop campaigns and activism around the issues you care about.

ALISTAIR MACKIE

The Trade Unionist and the Tycoon

I have known Alistair Mackie for 30 years. He was born in Canada and brought up in Ayrshire after his family returned to their native Scotland. Alistair contracted tuberculosis, ending his ambition to go to university – only 4 per cent of young people went on to higher education at this time, very few of them from the type of working-class background that Alistair came from. After serving an apprenticeship as a compositor and junior reporter at his local newspaper, he went on to work on the Scottish Daily Express, *becoming a leading trade union figure.*

He came to prominence in the early 1970s when the Express *owners decided to close their Scottish titles. In response, Alistair and the rest of the workforce established a Workers' Committee to defend their jobs. In need of another investor to make workers' ownership a reality, in stepped the former MP, businessman Robert Maxwell, with a burning desire to take over a newspaper on the cheap.*

Following a brief period of co-operation there ensued a battle between the workers and Maxwell.

The story of the Scottish Daily News *is the story of a battle between workers' determination and one businessman's megalomania.*

Alistair Mackie is the embodiment of a Scottish working-class intellectual: a historian, a writer, a journalist, a tradesman, a trade unionist, a Burns scholar, a former council leader and a parliamentary candidate. He inspired me in my youth and encouraged many throughout his long and full life. He in his 90s and lives in Bathgate with his dog.

I WAS BORN in Canada, where my parents had emigrated for work. We returned when I was three and lived in Kilmarnock in Ayrshire, where I went to the Grange Academy. When I was a wee boy, I remember being told I was lucky to live in Ayrshire because many famous people came from the area – Robert Burns, William Wallace, Robert the Bruce, people like that.

I was brought up with a sense of history and have had a lifelong interest in the subject, in particular the work of Burns and the history of that time.

When I was at school, I had a great ambition and that was to go to university. It became a burning ambition, even as young boy of eight or nine, which was quite strange for a young, working-class boy at that time because very few people where I lived went to university.

To get to university you had to sit an examination to get into Kilmarnock Academy, so I sat and passed that exam and got into the high school. However, after two years I took tuberculosis, which was initially misdiagnosed resulting in me receiving no treatment. My ambition to study was scuppered, as it was impossible to study with my illness.

However, I managed to get a job at the local newspaper and it was the best thing I ever did.

I started my apprenticeship as a compositor and junior reporter in 1947. The Editor was a wee Glasgow hard man called John Hunter and he said to me on the first day, 'Right, son, the first thing you need to learn is, don't believe a word anyone tells you, you have to find out the truth yourself!' The stories I was sent out to get for him had to be the truth. Even if my mother and father had told me something different, he wanted me to ignore them in search of the unvarnished truth. And he wanted evidence to back up the story. It was a great lesson which I have carried with me my whole life.

I enjoyed working at the paper. It was a seven-year apprenticeship for a compositor, this was the method used to set the pages and create the metal plates from which the paper was printed. As an apprentice you were protected by the union but didn't get full membership until your time was out. I believed I had a job for life.

In 1952 I was called up for National Service in the Royal Air Force but during that time, my ill health returned, and the TB affected my kidneys badly. I was advised I only had four months to live but they agreed to experiment on me with a new drug called 'streptomycin', which saved my life. I was the first person in the UK to recover from renal TB because receiving this drug. I was very lucky.

After National Service I went back to my trade but again experienced further poor health with long periods in hospital, including an operation to have my right kidney removed – the other was left functioning with only 70 per cent efficacy. After that, I was discharged and told never to work again but that was not for me, I wanted to live a fulfilling life. I wanted to work, so I took a job at the *Daily Express* in Glasgow. It was a high pressure, intense job with the news coming in at a rapid pace. Very challenging, but my health actually improved. I loved the work.

By the time I joined the *Express* I was already a member of the Labour Party. I had joined in 1946 at around the age of 16 partly inspired by hearing Harold Laski speak about socialism at a Fabian Society meeting in my hometown. I joined with a different attitude to my parents. They believed the Labour Party was there to make things better for people, whereas my view was it was there to change the world. So, I adopted a Marxist view of the world, but I didn't want a revolution. I wanted radical social and economic change but not the violent overthrow of capitalism. I didn't like Soviet-style socialism which to me was socialist economics with a type of fascistic, dictatorial politics. I couldn't find a party that completely reflected my beliefs, so I lumped in with the Labour Party as being the nearest to my philosophy. And that has guided me all my life. I accepted Marxist philosophy and adapted it and applied it to any situation I came across in life. I still believe Marxism will evolve over time to determine the way we organise society.

After around three months at the *Express* I was asked to stand as the 'father of the chapel', the senior trade union official in my branch of the National Typographical Association in the case room, representing over 100 staff, the first non-Glasgow person to do so. It was a chapel where the Masonic lodge had a very heavy influence. Now I personally have nothing against Masons, but they should not have brought their Masonic practices into the workplace and certainly not into the trade union.

I was committed to equality and non-discrimination on grounds of race, religion, etc. Some people did not like the fact that I argued against the discrimination I saw against Roman Catholics in our union – we only had one

Catholic in our entire branch! The *Express* never really challenged this. In the two years I was in the role, I wanted to build a broad union alliance but in the *Express* you had various categories of worker – professionals (journalists), craftsmen (case room and stereo) tradesmen (electricians, engineers), clerical (typists, administrators), semi-skilled and unskilled (labourers, etc). It was ludicrous that there were five or six groups; this helped the company, not the workers. I tried to build a better relationship and get us working together and was criticised by some in our chapel for doing so. That summer I went on holiday and came back to discover I had been removed from my union role. As compensation, I was offered the job as chairman of the federated chapel, which previously was a weak position that only really existed to try and get a pension for all of us at the paper. I said I would do it but under new rules, which I wrote and were agreed, it meant I was allowed to go to meetings of every chapel or branch at the paper and take part in proceedings. This meant we could begin to develop a more unified approach to issues instead of everyone having a different view to put to management or chapels fighting against each other.

This 'imperial chapel' became strong and more coherent. These strange titles that are used in journalism come from the fact that, historically, printing and publishing came from monasteries and religious orders. That is where the terminology of 'chapels' and 'fathers' comes from, terms that are still used in the print and media sector.

Despite our growing unity, the owners of the paper were not prepared to move on the pensions issue, so we called a national meeting of all *Express* unions in Manchester, where we met together for the first time to discuss the matter and our demand for a sickness fund. I was voted in as the 'deputy grand imperial father' with around 10,000 staff members across the titles. We were now serious, and management knew it. To be honest, the management then were good, we had decent relations with them, and worked well together.

Things went along fairly well until the *Express* owners decided to close the Glasgow office. They said they were not making enough profit and had to close Glasgow or Manchester. I did not want any office closed and refused to throw the Manchester workers under a bus, so I argued forcefully for the retention of both. However, it was clear the decision had already been made to close the Glasgow office. The *Express* and *The Citizen* (the other title printed in Glasgow) were to go.

As a group of workers, we formed a Workers Action Committee compromising of around seven or eight senior union officers from across the papers to see what we could do to save jobs in Glasgow. Early on, I got a phone call from a senior Glasgow MP, Hugh Brown, who said to me, 'Have you thought about setting up a co-operative to take over the paper?'

Now I was quite embarrassed because I hadn't thought about a co-op, although I should have. I put the idea to the Action Committee and pointed out we could either go for the co-operative idea or the paper would shut within a month! That was the stark choice before us.

We made a statement saying we believed in a workers' co-operative, but because the Tories were in power, we knew we would get zero support. However just after that, there was a general election and Harold Wilson became Prime Minister. We met with him very quickly. He wanted support from people like us and politically it suited him and the more we looked at our plan for the workers to run the paper the more feasible it looked.

One of the big issues we had was trying to work out how many workers we needed to produce the *Express*; we had already conceded *The Citizen* would have to go. We agreed that we would go for it and Harold Wilson gave us around about £2 million towards the venture. This was very ambitious for the government and it took a lot of persuading as the Civil Service tried to block it. They were telling him he could not do it. We had to be forceful.

We re-established the paper under a new name, *The Scottish Daily News*, and had full buy-in from all the chapels, except one, the journalists, who thought they were above everyone else and were not too keen. They wanted a paper led and controlled by them. They thought they were the only real professionals and the rest of us were just there to support them.

Eventually Robert Maxwell came in as a potential investor in the paper. I didn't want to meet him as he had a very bad reputation, but I had to meet him as he had the only serious offer on the table and we needed his cash injection. He offered 50 per cent of what the workers would put in from their redundancy (on average around about £3,000 each). But he wouldn't come in as an outsider, he would have to be part of it himself. I was doubtful about Maxwell, but he went public about his intention and we weren't really in a position to refuse. He then said he would have to be the chairman and I said, 'Not on your life.' I was the chairman at the time, so we made him vice chairman. Then he started telling us what to do and everything became a fight between us and Maxwell – it got very nasty. He wanted one thing: to own and control the paper. Of course, this went against everything we were trying to do as it would no longer be a workers' co-operative under his proposed regime.

We had some great journalists at the *Express*, but many were lured away and snapped up quickly by other papers, so we were left with those who couldn't get another job. Across the rest of paper we had very skilled people who knew what they were doing, but at an early stage we were aware of the poor quality of the journalism, although these people still held a lot of power and provided the power base behind Maxwell. They didn't like mixing with non-journalists;

likewise the craftspeople, who didn't like mixing with the tradesmen. This ran against the ethos of the paper that we were all in it together. It sounds absurd now, but that is how it was.

So, we produced the paper. We needed around 350,000 sales to break even and we got that for the first few weeks or so, but it then fell to around 200,000. The production of the paper was excellent and efficient, but the writing let it down repeatedly. I remember one day, one of the managers came in and said, 'I was reading a report in *The Scotsman* about last night's game between Rangers and Hearts and then I read the same story in our paper. I felt I was reading about a different game. Our report was so boring and uninteresting!' Well, that was confirmation for me of the poor journalism.

I tried to bring in outsiders to boost circulation, people like Mary Holland, a BBC journalist who was very good, but when she saw and heard how the journalists were treating people who came into the paper she said, 'Sorry I couldn't work with them.'

My deputy, Jimmy McNamara (father and grandfather of footballers Jackie Snr and Jnr), went to see the Editor. He said to him that we were entering a key stage of the paper's development and it was either Maxwell or Alistair that would be running the paper. Jimmy warned him it would not survive if it were left to Maxwell. After three months, Maxwell told journalists and the case room staff he would need to become the chairman, or the paper would collapse.

A meeting was called. I said, 'If you pass over the paper to Maxwell, you are destroying the principle of what we set out to do and that was to create a workers' co-operative. If you hand control to this rascal, cheat and liar he will destroy it! You won't stay alive because he doesn't want the paper to stay alive.' And with that, I resigned. My deputies and supporters were all removed, and Maxwell took sole control.

After three weeks, it was clear things were going badly and I was asked to go back, but I refused. I said it would be better to let the paper die with dignity than allow Maxwell to dictate. That is what happened. It was very sad. The concept was beautiful and the production of the paper was excellent, but we failed largely because we didn't have the quality of journalism to make it a good read and we had Maxwell trying to close it down for his selfish purposes.

The creation of a co-operative fitted with my political philosophy. Workers have the capacity to do anything they want to do, given the chance. Any worker has the ability to contribute to running their workplace for themselves. The workers are the experts, they are doing the job every day, so they can run it and own it successfully. It can be done. For example, we relaunched the paper, changing it from a broadsheet to a tabloid within four weeks. I spoke to the *Daily Mail* union who advised me it took them six months – we did it in four weeks, because there were no managers thinking they knew what they were doing. We had the workers in control and they knew exactly what they had to do.

The demise of the *News* was not the end of my dealings with Maxwell. Years after the paper collapsed, I got a phone call from a friend at the *Daily Record* who told me that Maxwell was taking over *The Record* and *The Mirror* and that he wanted to close them down, and that if they kept it quiet, they would get decent redundancy pay.

I told my pal, 'Do not trust him one bit, you will get nothing from him. You are free to criticise him, and you have a duty to tell the public what his plans are.'

He did that and went public with it. Once it was out there, I was invited on to STV to discuss Maxwell and how he would deal with the workforce, because I had previous experience of him. The reporter asked me what I thought of him. I said, 'He is a cheat and a liar and you can never trust him. The people at *The Record* will find that out for themselves.' The reporter said, 'But he was colleague of yours.'

I said, 'What do you mean?'

He replied, 'Well, he is a socialist!'

I said, 'What? Don't be ridiculous. Hitler claimed to be socialist, as did Joseph Stalin. Maxwell comes into *that* category of socialist.'

A few days afterwards, I was at a council meeting in Linlithgow (I was leader of the West Lothian Council by then) and one of the council staff came in and said that my wife was on the phone for me. I knew something must be up, as she would never phone me at work unless it was very urgent. She told me two lawyers representing Robert Maxwell had appeared at the door. I asked her what they wanted, and she said, 'A million pounds – you are being sued by Robert Maxwell.'

I said, 'Well there's a jar above the cooker with about a tenner's worth of coins in it, give them that and tell them that's all we've got.'

However, it was true he was suing STV and me – not for saying he was 'a cheat and a rogue' but because I compared him to 'Stalin and Hitler'. Within a fortnight, STV struck a deal with him and settled, leaving me high and dry.

I knew if it came to court, it would be very costly. I was quoted around £25,000 for legal representation. I have never had £25,000 in my life. There was no question of me employing a lawyer at that cost, so I would have to represent myself in court. I spoke to a woman at the Court of Session who advised me I would have to come in every day to see if Maxwell had submitted his precognition statement and when he had I could submit mine. I said, 'I can't come in every day. I am leader of West Lothian District Council, I've got work to do.' She agreed to sign me in each day and alert me once Maxwell's precognition has come in. I got help from a local lawyer, John Teague, to write up my statement and submit it to the court.

Things went on for about a year and three months. During that time, I built up a decent rapport with Maxwell's lawyers. One phoned me to say, 'Alistair, your mad friend from Oxford [Maxwell] has been on the phone. He has changed his precognition.' He advised me to look at the first and second statements Maxwell had submitted and said, 'You have a very strong defence; I won't point out the differences in the case, that would be unfair to my client, but you will see for yourself.' They clearly had no time for Maxwell.

In the meantime, and completely by chance, I was at a council function and met a chap who had owned a printing and publishing business in Edinburgh. He told me he knew Maxwell from their time in the Army. Maxwell had previously told me he was in the Royal Artillery and had been put in this regiment as they didn't want him in the infantry, where he would have a greater chance of being captured and murdered by the Nazis because of his Jewish background. He had less chance of that in the artillery. The chap I spoke to had been a major in the artillery after the war and was in Berlin when the British Army went into the city. He said he was only there a few weeks when he was told of a group of British soldiers who were engaged in blackmarketeering. The major was dispatched to arrest them and found the leader of the gang was none other than Sergeant Robert Maxwell. They were all charged and sent to the glasshouse for six months and then, according to this man, dishonourably discharged from the Army. Soon after this, Maxwell published a book claiming he was a captain of an elite infantry regiment and recalled all of his glorious wartime memories. I thought, this is good enough for me. I was sitting on the information the ex-major had given me.

As time marched on, I was told I had to submit my defence to the court, as the trial was due to take place in four weeks. I submitted my papers and listed a number of people I was going to call as witnesses, including the former major. Maxwell's lawyers asked for the name of this witness, but I withheld it and simply said to them, 'Ask Robert Maxwell, he will know who he is.'

They said, 'I think you are playing a dangerous game, Mr Mackie.'

'Well, so be it,' I replied.

A week or so later, I got a letter saying there would be no court case and the whole thing died a death. Soon afterwards, Maxwell's lawyer phoned me to say, 'Okay Alistair, the case is withdrawn and it can't be brought back, but just as a matter of interest, what is the name of the former major you cited?'

I said, 'It doesn't matter, he died 18 months ago.'

When I look back on that time, I would say that it taught me a lot. I think the main thing is that I would urge everyone to become involved in things. Get involved in your union, if you are not a member of one, then join. Involve yourself in your work, because you spend a big part of your life there. You are creating something, so take a real interest, make it better and your working life will be more fulfilling. Try and bring the management on board so that everyone can work together to make our working lives better.

Time is the greatest thing you can give to anything or anyone. We only have a limited amount of it and giving it is a huge gift. If we give that to our employers, they should give something back in return. We are not slaves and should never be regarded as slaves – we should all be seen as co-producers.

I believe, in time, workers will own the means of production – be it a factory or office, business or shop, or whatever – because I think it just makes sense.

For now, we should all make our contribution in preparation for a time when society moves towards a more socialist or Marxist model with workers in control. I do not want a violent revolution, but I think a common sense move to such a scenario will happen. The alternative is slavery and exploitation.

The children who work in slavery, or who do not have an education or food, they are my children too. They are all our children and we have a responsibility to them. We can make a difference. That is why I believe in working together to address these issues. It is why I believe in the European Union and why I ultimately want to see world government. I believe in co-operation.

If politicians learn anything from the shambles of Brexit, it is this: the leaders of the EU and world leaders must become more accountable to the people they claim to represent. If they do not heed this, then we will see division, alienation and conflict.

I am optimistic for the future, because there is an alternative to the status quo where power and wealth lie in the hands of a tiny elite while the other 99 per cent struggle to get by. That is an outrageous situation. There is a real alternative in socialism. In our society, we need to encourage people to think. When I was a councillor, I remember speaking to a gathering of teachers along with another councillor, who said we educated people so that they could get a job and contribute to the economy. I disagreed entirely, because I believe we should educate young people, so they can enjoy a Shakespeare play or Mozart's music or a piece of poetry or talk about art and history and politics. Education should be about making people think, making them aware of the world we live in and how they can contribute to it. That is my ambition for the young people of today.

Alistair Mackie was forced to wait until Robert Maxwell died to publish his story of The Scottish Daily News *in his book* The Trade Unionist and the Tycoon.

Bathgate No More...

Jim Swan is a well-known figure in the Scottish trade union movement. I met him as a young activist in the Labour Party and West Lothian Trades Council and we went on to establish a lasting friendship. He taught me a lot when I served as his deputy while both of us were councillors in West Lothian in the early 2000s. He is a straightforward man with no hidden agenda – all he wants is for people to be treated fairly, with dignity and respect.

The British Leyland motor plant at Bathgate was established in 1962 to build vans, trucks and tractors. The site was huge, dominating the local community and economy. It had its own training school, a major apprenticeship programme and a supply chain employing a vast number of people.

Jim Swan served his apprenticeship as an engineer in the machine shops of the Central Scotland's industrial heartland. He failed the health test when called up for National Service but went on to join the merchant navy. As a skilled fitter, he then started work at the British Motor Corporation plant (later renamed British Leyland) at Bathgate. He was a shop steward before being elected plant union convener and was responsible for around 6,000 members at the peak of employment. As Thatcher began dismantling the UK's manufacturing capacity, with Leyland and the well organised workforce firmly in her sights, Bathgate became a key battleground. Jim Swan was in the heart of the battle.

I WAS BORN in Harthill, North Lanarkshire in 1939 – my dad said I started the war. We experienced things then that were tough but stood us in good stead for the rest of our lives. I lived through rationing, which made us appreciative of the food we eat today and things we might otherwise take for granted. There were four of us but one of my sisters died when she was very young.

I went to the local primary school, then the junior secondary, where I enjoyed technical subjects. Through my cousins and uncles, I got an apprenticeship in Coatbridge at an engineering factory called Murray & Paterson. It was a strange place; they still had the skylights painted black from the wartime blackouts. Many of their machines were old, still running on belts, but we got good training and a very good apprenticeship. It was a general engineering firm, producing everything from a needle to an anchor – we really did do anchors.

As a third-year apprentice I was given the blueprints to a job and told: 'All the castings are in the yard and the cranes are ready to move them for you. Get them in, mark then off, process them through the machine shop and complete the sub-assembly to a full fit.' It was tremendous experience. We made the rollers, the chokes and other items for the huge Ravenscraig Steel plant – the 'Craig – in nearby Motherwell. I enjoyed that work and went on to machine tool maintenance. I liked that but after my apprenticeship finished I was called up for National Service. However, when I was x-rayed they found a shadow on my lung and they failed me. This was worrying, but I joined the merchant navy to work on the Royal Mail lines. Looking back on this experience, it showed the value of proactive health tests in identifying conditions that can be treated, before it's too late.

There I learned about the class divide – the officers didn't speak to or mix with the lower orders like us. I joined the Curry Line, based in Leith. The difference was stark. Once, the ship docked in Liverpool and we went to see a boxing match. We all went, the captain, the chief engineer, the pantry boy and me; we worked and socialised as a team. I liked that way of working.

When I got married, I left the navy and joined Pickering's in Wishaw. The wages were poor. I can remember my wife and I saying if we could only get £20 per week we would be in clover. In 1965 I joined British Leyland in Bathgate, not on £20 a week but on £19. In 1972, we had a seven-week strike. The factory opened on the 'district engineering rate' of pay, which was way below the rate paid to Leyland workers in England, so the '72 strike was about pay parity.

During that time, the miners were on strike too. They beat the Heath Government by sticking together and Leyland workers, or BMC as it was then, gave their support by blocking the lorries from going into the power stations. That was solidarity in action.

I joined the Labour Party in the '60s and was an active member of the Amalgamated Engineering Union. At that time, we had 6,000 people working at the plant in Bathgate, over 1,000 in our branch all on check off with their subs paid to branch from payroll.

I was the shop steward in the tool room. One of the first disputes I was involved in as a steward was not about money, it was about health and safety. We wanted safety glasses, steel toe capped boots, overalls. These were basics, but we didn't have them.

In '74, the Labour Government brought in the Health and Safety at Work Act, a wonderful advance in workplace safety. The TUC trained the safety reps and they became better versed in health and safety than the company's appointed person. As a branch, we bought 100 copies of the book *Hazards at Work*, which set things out in layman's terms for all our reps. We now knew about things like damaging decibel levels, so we campaigned for ear defenders. We learned about asbestos and forced major changes in practice when working with asbestos. The fitters and boilermakers got new equipment, but areas were not sealed off and people were still exposed to asbestos dust. I became close to people like Frank McGuire from Thompsons Solicitors, who worked with us and educated us on everything to do with asbestos. Frank was brilliant.

The company had by this time changed its name to 'British Leyland' and when Thatcher took over as Prime Minister she introduced the 'Edwards Plan', supposedly to address problems in the business and make it more efficient. The reality is, all he did was flog off the profitable parts of the business, leaving the problematic parts.

We had put in a lot of work on a new tractor and managed to do in six months what would normally have taken 18. The tractor passed all its tests and went on sale at Smithfield Market. Soon after this, all the stewards were called to a meeting, where one of the senior managers said trade was not so good and he looked at his watch and said, 'By my watch, five minutes ago we just sold the entire rights to the tractor and its production to Marshall Tractors.' Everyone in the room went quiet. I stood up and said, 'No way!'

We then gathered as a group of shop stewards and I said, 'We can't just go on strike over this, the men are not up for it. We will have to be careful and think about what we do.'

Thatcher saw the British Leyland car workers as well organised and wanted to take us on. We called a mass meeting and said to the workers, 'We want you to give the union "a fighting pound a week". This will allow us to use your money to organise properly and stop any tractor going to Marshall Tractors. We will keep them here.' And for weeks, we did that.

The men who refused to move and transport the tractors were taken off the clock by management, so the union paid them from the fighting fund. The shop stewards took over control of distribution and stopped materials going out. The workers at a plant in England came out on strike over a similar issue with lorry testing. However, instead of coming out on strike, we decided to occupy the factory and leaked this to the press, who turned up in big numbers. We had agreed between us who would walk out and who would stay behind to work as part of the occupation. We locked down the plant and out came a fleet of the new 'harvest gold' painted tractors to block off C Block with big banners saying 'No Harvest Gold for Marshall's.' The BBC news and the papers were full of the story. We were now locked in.

The company had left people in to ensure we did not cause damage, but we had no intention of causing damage as this was our factory and our jobs we were fighting for.

A few weeks earlier, I had been with Ina Scott, the union convener at the nearby Plessey Electronics factory, which was also under threat of closure. I had told her about my plan to occupy the factory. A few hours after we locked the gates at Bathgate, the phone went for me in the union office and the voice on the phone sang 'anything you can do, we can do better.' It was Ina who told me, 'We have just occupied the factory too.'

Just as they did that, the Plessey boiler broke down, so we got our boilermakers to go and fix it and in return, Ina and her team came to our canteen and cooked stovies for us all.

We had been locked in for two months when we heard we were going to be served with legal papers to get us out. We said, 'If they come for us, we should end the occupation and immediately go on strike.' The local economy was in trouble and we knew we had to win to save the factory. The union leadership asked us to have a mass meeting, so we did. Hugh Wyper from the union leadership addressed the men and so did I, then we put it to a vote. 'Do we go back or not?' It was 50/50.

Hugh said, 'You can't stay out on 50/50.' So, we went back. At this time, I used to run to work and one morning as I was going through the gate, the security guy showed me the front page of *The Express*. The headline read: 'Bathgate to Close!' I was stunned.

I went straight into the managing director's office and said to him, 'Can you hear anything?'

He said, 'No. How?'

'Good, because nothing will be done in the plant until you explain this.'

He looked stunned. I don't think he knew this was how the closure would be communicated to the workers.

I said, 'Is this how you tell thousands of people and their families they are losing their jobs?'

The next day we had held a mass meeting and the stewards called everybody out and reoccupied the factory.

When the police were called, they said they could only remove us via a court order and went away. This occupation lasted for another two months.

The government and management wanted to close the factory quickly, but we got two more years out of it. During that time, we supported the miners by refusing to take scab coal. We helped a group of young boys who had been sacked by a contractor for a bit of high jinks, stopping the loading of freight until they were reinstated, and they were. The union controlled the closure of the factory instead of allowing it to happen at breakneck speed.

All through this period, we worked very closely with our local MP, Tam Dalyell, who gave us unremitting support. He helped us in so many ways – on one occasion forcing Secretary of State, George Younger, who was on his way to Aberdeen, to stop at Edinburgh to meet Tam and a deputation of District and Regional councillors. The result was the Scottish Office had to try and put together a package to support the local economy. The shop stewards and me as convener weren't allowed to attend. We demanded to speak to them, but eventually we only got to speak to the senior civil servant in charge. This showed the Tories' disdain for working people.

Part of the plan put forward was the reopening of the Bathgate to Edinburgh and Glasgow rail line, a new junction onto the M8 motorway and action to address the Avon Gorge road, a long-standing problem. This package was submitted as a plan to open up the West Lothian economy and create new jobs.

As we were leaving, the senior civil servant called back Jimmy Wallace and me and said, 'Mr Swan, I cannot save your members' jobs. All I can do is try to help create new ones for your sons and daughters.'

Well, we knew then the factory was doomed.

In spite of this, we fought on and went down to see the owners of JCB to put forward our plan to save jobs and the business. I proposed that they took over the engine plant and let us keep production going.

Their leading man said, 'Mr Swan, you have been very honest with us. I would take over your plant if I got many millions of pounds like the government are giving the Japanese to come and set up here.'

He then took us round the factory and we had a very good, intelligent discussion about the use of new flexible machinery. He was surprised that he and I were on the same page about the adoption of new advanced manufacturing technology and that I knew the impact this could have on production.

There was then a discussion about saving the engine plant at Bathgate and doing a deal with Cummins but all along, the Leyland senior management were stringing us along and telling us lie after lie.

The press swung in behind us when they too found the management to be lying. We never got a deal with any other partner or owner, the reality being that the government wanted Bathgate closed completely and in 1986 that is what happened, although for a while after some spares were made there.

I left in September 1986. It was all very sad. All those who thought they would pick up a redundancy cheque and a job right away found that the pit had closed, Plessey was closing and there was 25 per cent unemployment in some wards in West Lothian. We knew that was going to happen, that is why we fought so hard to save the factory.

I never worked in engineering again, but I did get a job at the Lothian Trade Union Resource Centre, which brought together the Trades Councils from East, West and Midlothian and Edinburgh. This project was supposed to run for four years – it ran for 25. We did a lot of advice work, testing for industrial diseases such as hearing loss; we ran health and safety education courses and welfare rights and employment advice sessions. We introduced International Workers' Memorial Day to Scotland – there are now services every year across the UK. And we developed the Hazards movement and Occupational Health networks.

I was then elected on to West Lothian Council, where we developed a lot of policy initiatives on the environment and health and safety. We became UK Council of the Year in 2006.

Looking back over my years of activism, I learned many things. As an apprentice, we went on strike for an extra holiday and won; nothing can devalue that extra day we got. In Leyland, we fought and won a sick pay scheme, which kicked in after three days of sickness. Some of our members complained, saying the office staff get it after one day, they should be put on three days like us. My argument was, 'No, we will campaign for it after one day just like them.' You do not advance your cause as a worker by taking away the hard-won gains of a fellow worker. You should always try to race to the top, not the bottom. We got the sick pay scheme set up and then a pension scheme. These advances were fought for, negotiated and won by the union for all our members. The fact that people get paid holidays, have the right to join a pension scheme and other basic rights at work remain because of the actions of people years gone by. Of course, every time the Tories come into power they try to weaken or dismantle these rights, and it will be up to a Labour government to once again bring about, as John McDonnell has said, 'a revolution in workers' rights.'

I recall Jimmy Milne, the then STUC (Scottish Trades Union Congress) general secretary saying to me, 'If you want to win a campaign, don't put all your eggs in one basket. If you are fighting a cause, you need the community behind you. If you can bind in other parties then your case will so much stronger.' I have always tried to reach out and build such support across the community and grow support for the causes I believe in. Building unity is always the best approach.

TERRY RENSHAW

The Shrewsbury 24

As a former construction worker, I took a close interest in the Shrewsbury 24 case. My da, who, like me, was a bricklayer, took part in the only national building workers strike in the early '70s. Conditions on sites then were dreadful, health and safety almost non-existent and pay for skilled work poor. These were Victorian working conditions that had barely changed in a century – workers had had enough and they decided to act.

With no private wealth or assets to draw upon, all that working people have to sell to keep a roof over their head and their families fed is their labour. Collective action, protest and the withdrawal of labour is a huge step that no one takes lightly. It means a loss of pay and can result in the sack. Trade union organising in the transient construction sector is never easy. The mass action of building workers across the UK during the early '70s was unprecedented. And what happened to 24 joiners, plasterers, steel erectors and painters in the aftermath of a peaceful day of lawful picketing at Shrewsbury in 1972, where not one arrest or act of violence took place, was beyond extraordinary.

Terry Renshaw and his comrades were subjected to the full weight of the political, judicial and media establishment. No trick was too dirty to be played to ensure that the truth never came to light – but it did.

This the remarkable case of the Shrewsbury 24.

I WAS BORN in a little village in North Wales, where I still live. My mother worked in munitions production during WW2. She looked after me, my sister and two brothers while my father was away serving the country. He died in World Cup year 1966 at the young age of 48, which was tragic for all of us. I went to secondary modern school and left with one qualification, in Art.

On leaving school, I managed to get a job doing general processing work with a branch of Cortaulds in a factory making nylon and other products. In 1964, I started an apprenticeship with the company as a painter and decorator at their plant at Greenfield in North Wales, where 7,000 people worked at its peak. I left in 1969 after my apprenticeship and went to work in the private sector. The first big job I was on was for J. Jarvis and Son, doing pebbledash, epoxy resins and the like on a big office block in Chester. When that finished, I went into the steel works doing subcontract work.

I was always involved in the trade union and by 1972 I was the branch chairman of the painters' and decorators' union, the ASP&D. The Union of Construction Workers and Allied Technical Trades (UCATT) had just formed in a coming together of the bricklayers', joiners' and painters' unions. At that time, one person was killed every day on construction sites in the UK. The conditions on site were very poor, as was pay. You got more pay in a supermarket than on site. A culmination of pay, health and safety and welfare issues brought things to a head. We couldn't go on seeing building workers getting 'murdered' every day – I use that term deliberately as I believe it was 'murder'.

The building trade is a nomadic industry. You work on a site then, when the job is finished, you pack up and head for the next site, looking for work wherever that may be.

In 1972, we set up *The Building Workers' Charter*, a rank and file produced newspaper that we distributed on sites across the country. The *Charter* carried a set of demands developed by workers on sites and acted as a pressure group on full-time officials in UCATT, the GMB and TGWU. The *Charter* was brought together by the men on the ground and we were very vocal in telling our officials what we wanted. We negotiated with the National Federation of Building Trade Employers, raising issues identified within the *Charter*.

Around the same time, five dockers were locked up in Pentonville prison for trade union activity – they became known as the Pentonville Five. Every building site stopped work in support of the dockers and the official solicitor had to turn up at Pentonville to release them.

The demands of the *Charter* were:

- 30 for 35 (meaning £30 a week for 35 hours' work),
- Improved health and safety,

- Improved welfare on site,
- And action against 'the lump'.

'The lump' was a like a cancer creeping into the industry. This was where workers got a lump sum for a piece of work, which appeared to be a good rate, but they never got any sick pay, holiday pay or anything like that. It was a con. 'Kill the lump' became one of our slogans. Securing better welfare provision on site was essential: we wanted drying rooms, toilets, canteens, etc. The reality for many workers was that they would be working outside in the pouring rain and they would either have to go home and get changed, losing pay, or work on, wet and freezing cold. There was usually no toilet on sites. If you had to go, you went behind a shed, behind a tree or bush, down in a foundation, anywhere. It was primitive.

As our pressure increased, UCATT had a special conference where there was a call for a national strike in support of the aims of the Charter. At the start of the dispute, action was targeted with specific sites identified. In July of '72, selective action started with the men on the sites not identified for action contributing financially to help pay the ones who were on strike. After a few weeks, we could see this wasn't having the desired impact, as some sites that were supposed to be closed down continued working. It was too ad hoc. The Charter movement met as a national group and declared an all-out strike. It was the first and only national building strike in UK history. Interestingly, UCATT never called an all-out strike and officials tried to claim it wasn't official action, but in our eyes, it was unofficial for the selective sites but official for the all-out action. The men came out quite readily once we explained the situation. We visited lots of sites, speaking to groups of workers about the dispute and our demands.

After the first few weeks of the strike, I went into hospital for an operation that went wrong. I was out of action for a few weeks but in my absence my colleagues were very active. Today, we see building sites fenced off with hoardings all round them, but then it was open field where people could walk on from anywhere, so we organised teams of activists to go on site and speak directly to the bricklayers, joiners, painters and the rest. There was no traditional picket line to try and manage. We would go on and find the site cabin and ask the agent if we could speak to the men. We would bring them together and make an appeal for them to join the strike.

Nationally, discussions were ongoing to try and bring an end to the dispute – our national officer, Albert Prest, represented us but in our opinion he wasn't advancing our cause one bit.

In week 11, I was recovering from being hospital and wanted out the house because I was bored. The Chester and North Wales action group used to meet up in the Bull & Stirrup pub in Chester to discuss tactics. Colleagues from Oswestry asked if we would give them support to target sites that were still working in Shropshire area. The committee agreed to help out. On September 6th 1972, we hired four or five coaches for the journey. People came from Wrexham, Flint and the Chester area. We all met up at Oswestry Labour Club to discuss where we were going and which sites to target. We didn't know until we met at the club what the plan was.

The first site we went to was called Kingswood a small housing development on the A5. We sent out Des Warren and a few others to speak to the site agent, who then appeared with a loaded shotgun! He told us to clear off or we would 'get both barrels'. At that, some of the other lads gave support. The gun was taken from the agent without being fired. The barrels were cracked open, the cartridges removed and the gun given to the police officers who had appeared. The police then said they would take us to every site we wanted to go to. From Kingswood onwards, we had motorcycle outriders and officers on the coaches directing us to each site. At one point, there were about 70 or 80 police officers with us. At no time did they express concern about what we were doing. They never took anyone's name, they didn't arrest or caution a single person, it was all very straightforward and good-natured.

Of all seven sites we visited, only one, Brookside, was identified in the later court case. This was a Sir Robert McAlpine site. McAlpine was the treasurer of the Tory Party and had a direct line to Robert Carr, the then Home Secretary. Even on this site, no arrests were made. There were occasional heated exchanges with those who wanted to continue working, and on one site a newly built wall was pushed over, but there was no violence or fisticuffs. Photos taken by the *Shropshire Star* showed the men in a huddle being addressed by us, the police standing back, arms folded and sleeves rolled up, enjoying the sunshine. At the end of the day, Superintendent Meredith from West Mercia Police, who was in charge, came to us and said as his parting words, 'Okay, lads, you've had good days picketing. Thank you for the way you have behaved. Safe journey home.' We had been out all day and went straight home.

By week 13 the strike was over and the agreement reached gave us almost everything we had asked for. Pay, welfare and health and safety all improved dramatically. Indeed, a year or two later we had the introduction of the Health and Safety at Work Act and there is no doubt this was influenced heavily by our action and demands.

We all went back to work but rumours went around that the police had been asking questions about the strike and what had happened at Shrewsbury. Five months later, on Valentine's Day 1973, police from West Mercia swooped on houses across North Wales and arrested people for their involvement in the strike and actions at Shrewsbury. I was arrested and taken to Flint Police Station. Ricky Tomlinson was taken to Shrewsbury, as was Des Warren. We were all questioned separately and shown photographs taken by the *Shropshire Star*. They wanted to know the identities of the people in those photographs and what role they played on the day. They suggested, because I was a big lad, that I would have threatened people – which I didn't. One said, 'I have a good mind to beat you up here in this station!'

I said, 'You might have a mind to do it, but you wouldn't, would you?'

Shortly after, we got charge sheets through the post. I couldn't believe what they were saying we did. I was charged with *Conspiracy to intimidate people to abstain from lawful employment, affray and unlawful assembly*. No charges of violence or anything else. I noticed right away that the date of the charges was the date I was in hospital for my operation. They had put the wrong date. I did not tell a soul about this.

There was one committal hearing for all 24 of us. Then Lord Hailsham got involved and changed the law on jury selection for this trial – only for this trial. We now couldn't challenge the occupation of jurors on conflict of interest grounds. He did this unilaterally when Parliament was in recess.

The authorities split the trials up into three separate hearings. Warren and others versus the Crown, Murray and others versus the Crown and Renshaw and others versus the Crown. This was deliberate, so we couldn't go to each and give evidence in support of our co-accused.

In December '73 the first trial ended and saw Des Warren, Ricky Tomlinson and John McKinsie Jones go to jail, found guilty of all charges. At one point, Des Warren argued in court that his phone had been tapped. The judge said, 'We don't do that in this country. What makes you think your phone has been tapped?'

Des said, 'Well, I haven't paid the bloody bill for two years and it still hasn't been cut off.'

The second trial was January 1974 – three went to jail.

My trial was set to start in February '74. Roy Ward, my barrister, told me, 'They have you down as Des Warren's right-hand man and if you don't plead guilty you are going down for three years.' I refused to plead guilty, so they put an extra charge of Unlawful Assembly on me and an extra charge of Affray was added on the day I attended court. You couldn't do that now.

I missed the start of my trial as I had broken my leg ice-skating and was again in hospital. My barrister gave my apologies. The judge said, 'Check with the hospital if he is fit to travel and if he is, get him here in the morning.' I had to have three court ushers moving me around the courtroom.

As the trial proceeded, I played my trump card and pointed out the wrong date on the charge sheet. The judge asked, 'Why didn't you tell your defence counsel about this before now?'

I said, 'Because if I had he would probably have told the prosecution counsel, who would have tried to have cut a deal.'

The judge had to dismiss these charges, but I was convicted on the added ones. Eight of us were tried and all given suspended sentences – no one went to jail in our trial.

During this period, the union wouldn't back us because we were up on criminal charges, but across the country rank and file building workers and ordinary union members raised hundreds of thousands of pounds to pay our court fees, to support our families. I was a single man, so it didn't matter as much to me, but those who went to jail were financially supported all through that time. It was amazing how the rank and file workers stood with us all the way.

For the convicted there was an appeal supposed to be heard by Justice Salmond, but it ended up being heard by Lord Widgery, who had headed the Bloody Sunday tribunal. The newspapers presented us as the lowest of the low. Hundreds of police officers lined to the streets around the courtroom during the trials. The public must have been wondering, 'Who are these people?' In the media, we were portrayed as monsters.

Des and Ricky were treated appallingly in jail. Des was in 17 different prisons in three years. His wife, with their five kids, would go to Lincoln prison to visit, only to be told he'd been moved to Nottingham. Ricky was in 12 different prisons.

They went to prison on the 19th of December. We sent a Christmas card from the action committee with a message saying, 'We will be with you at Christmas', meaning with them in spirit. What did the authorities do? They moved him just a few days after being sentenced, because they thought we were going to picket the prison. They were obsessed, they were totally obsessed and paranoid and believed we were all communists. Des was the only one of us who was in the Communist Party. A number of us were members of the Labour Party but it was communism the authorities were obsessed with.

When Ricky and Des were in jail as political prisoners they refused to comply and wear prison clothes, so they were put in solitary confinement for most of the time. Des was repeatedly and against his will given injections of drugs. He was treated terribly and was later diagnosed with drug-induced Parkinson's disease. When he came out he had no life and was stuck in a wheelchair until his death in 2004 aged around 62.

Over the years, I wrote to UCATT and urged them to take up the campaign for justice for the imprisoned workers. In 2003, under the 30-year rule, we asked to see the Cabinet papers from the trial. We were told we couldn't get them because to do so posed 'a threat to national security'. (David Blunkett as Home Secretary extended the date for publication by a further ten years.)

By 2006 our campaign group were meeting up regularly to plan the way ahead. We did the rounds of union and Labour Party branches, TUC conferences and the like. I took part in the 2008 Labour Party Conference crime and justice debate. I opened with the words: 'Terry Renshaw, UCATT, speaking to you as a convicted criminal.' The place went quiet as I spoke to them about Shrewsbury, our campaign and being a 'threat to national security'. The newspapers all wanted to interview me afterwards. On my way to the media room, I passed Jack Straw who was preparing for a book signing.

I said to him, 'Jack, as a politician you're no good – a little bit worse than useless.' He looked at me for a second and went back to his books.

He refused to talk to us over the years of our campaign.

In 2010, the coalition government came in and promised transparency in government and that if a petition on any matter got 100,000 signatures Parliament would debate the issue. The Hillsborough Campaign was one of the early ones to succeed in securing the 100,000. We used Ricky Tomlinson's celebrity status to get our petition going. All the big unions supported us and we got thousands of members to sign up, but as we watched the total number was decreasing, not increasing. We called the Cabinet office who said it was a glitch in the system!

We then started a paper petition and got people to sign up and return them to a PO Box, but when we checked the mailbox there was nothing there. A friendly CWU member went looking for them and found bags that had been stashed away. In the end, we got over 100,000 signatures and served the petition to Number 10 in December 2013. Meanwhile, Dave Anderson, MP for Blaydon, got a backbench debate on the release of the papers. A number of MPs weighed in supporting us. During the debate, one of the Tories claimed we had killed someone at Shrewsbury. Well, that was taking parliamentary privilege a bit too far – it was an out and out lie of the worst kind. At the end of the debate, the vote was 120 for the release of the papers with 3 against. The Tories still refused to release them. The Labour MPs involved did a brilliant job that day and went out to vote singing 'The Red Flag'.

We still haven't seen the papers. Some suggest they won't shed any light on things but Eileen Turnbull, our fantastic researcher, can almost predict what they will say as she has all the papers before and after, but not in the middle.

In April 2012, we served new evidence with the Criminal Cases Review Commission. A case officer and commissioner were appointed to look at the papers, both of whom were then taken off the case, only for the next two appointed to be taken off the case as well, until finally we got a letter from the 2017 appointee saying that our evidence didn't give grounds to go back to the Court of Appeal. This was a real kick in the guts.

We discussed the outcome with our solicitor, Jamie Potter, who advised us to go for a judicial review of the CCRC decision. We got a barrister's opinion from Danny Freedman, who agreed. However, we were made aware that if the CCRC won, they could come for around £150,000 from us. Of course, we didn't have that kind of money.

We thought long and hard about what to do and then met with Howard Beckett and Len McCluskey at UNITE, who said they would help, as did UNISON, PCS and other unions. Taking our case back to court was a huge step for us to take.

The hearing was called for 9th November 2018, before Justice Jay. The CCRC were so confident in their case they didn't send anyone to defend. Danny Freedman was on his feet for two hours, putting forward our case and taking questions from the judge. The judge retired to read his notes before returning and advising us that we had permission to go forward for a full judicial review before two appeal court judges in spring 2019. The CCRC were given 35 days to respond and did so – on the 35th day – saying they would challenge it. The case was set for Birmingham on the 30th of April.

On the day, we all turned up at court, but I couldn't see the case listed. Eileen Turnbull then told me that they were saying the court for our case was double booked! How on earth can a court be double booked? Anyway, the judge for our case said he was having that courtroom and the other case would have to take place elsewhere. We agreed the case could run on into the evening, so that we could finish it in a day instead of a day and half.

Danny Freeman started to present our case. At 11.50am, the CCRC barrister rose to his feet and asked, 'When are we thinking of breaking for lunch?'

'One o'clock,' said the judge.

The CCRC barrister then requested a recess.

We thought he needed the toilet.

The judge agreed to a recess.

We wondered what was going on.

When the hearing resumed, the CCRC barrister announced, 'I have consulted with my clients and I wish to concede the case.'

It was a simple as that. We couldn't believe it.

He followed up by saying, 'I would like you (the judge) to give the case back to us so that we can reconsider our decision.'

The judge said he was 'of a mind to do so, but only if a new commissioner looks at it and you return with the proper decision.'

He was more or less telling them if they didn't make the decision themselves, the case would go back to the Court of Appeal. We are now still waiting on CCRC coming back to us with a date to return to the court of appeal. I hope that if that happens the Government (whichever party is in power) will offer no defence of the case.

So that is where we are.

Throughout all of this I have learned many things but the most important is the truth of the old cliché 'unity is strength'. One voice will not be heard but a thousand voices will be heard. That is why I am such a committed trade unionist.

Justice in this country is not what it professes to be – you can only get justice if you can pay for it. Without the financial support we have received we wouldn't be where we are.

On 23 March 2021, the Court of Appeal quashed the charges against the Shrewsbury pickets. In his ruling overturning the convictions, Lord Justice Fulford said: 'By the standards of today, what occurred was unfair to the extent that the verdicts cannot be upheld.'

After 47 years, the Shrewsbury pickets were cleared.

BRIAN FILLING

Mandela and Me

Brian Filling is an activist, socialist, geologist, educator, trade unionist, Honorary Doctor of Laws, and Honorary Consul for South Africa in Scotland.
I knew of Brian but before researching this book I had never met him. The hours I spent interviewing him were fascinating. Brian is a man who commands respect and in a quiet, dignified way exudes authority and confidence. There is little doubt that Brian was a key player in developing the strategy and building the activism internationally that brought about Mandela's release.

Brian was born, raised and educated in Glasgow. Following university, he was elected Editor of Challenge, *the Young Communist League (YCL) journal and went to London, where he was active in international solidarity campaigns. On returning to Scotland, he became the founding chair of the Scottish Committee of the Anti-Apartheid Movement, from 1976 until its dissolution, with the ending of apartheid, in 1994. He is chair of the successor organisation, Action for Southern Africa (ACTSA) Scotland and chair of the Nelson Mandela Scottish Memorial Foundation. Throughout the apartheid era,*

Brian helped to build and organise the anti-apartheid campaign in Scotland. He played a prominent role in persuading Glasgow City Council to grant the Freedom of the City to Mandela, then still a prisoner – a decision that inspired hundreds of cities worldwide to do the same thing.

In 1994, he was a guest in Pretoria at the Inauguration of Nelson Mandela as President of the Republic of South Africa. In 2012, he was awarded the National Order of Companions by Oliver Tambo at a ceremony in Tshwane (Pretoria). This is the highest honour bestowed on non-South Africans by the Republic of South Africa.

Here, he recalls his work as an anti-apartheid activist: starting from a small base, he helped build a global movement that brought about the release of Mandela and his fellow freedom fighters, and the end of the apartheid system.

I GOT INVOLVED in opposing apartheid, not through a big bang moment, but through the influence of my family, political education, reading, activism and meeting people struggling against imperialism, including many South African exiles. I came to understand that apartheid was a crime against humanity and learned that it was supported by all the western capitalist powers.

I was born in 1946 in Glasgow and have spent most of my life here, with a spell in London for a few years. I attended Temple Primary and Knightswood Comprehensive, both state schools. Then, after a short interlude when I went hitchhiking abroad, I studied at Glasgow University, graduating with a degree in Geology. Following graduation, I worked for IBM as a systems analyst/computer programmer in the very early days of computing.

Coming from a socialist family, I had a political background, so from an early age I understood the anti-colonial struggle. On my mother's side, my great grandfather, Robert Chambers, had been a delegate at the founding conference of the Scottish Trade Union Congress and my grandfather, Rab Chambers, also a trade unionist, was a founder of the Socialist Sunday School. My father was the chairman of the local Constituency Labour Party and my mother was an active member of the Communist Party. My grandfather used to take me to the Socialist Sunday School. He was one of the leading speakers at the various groups.

While I was working at IBM, I was elected editor of *Challenge*, the Young Communist League magazine. I had been in the YCL from the age of 13 and joined the Communist Party of Great Britain (CPGB) at 18.

I went to London with the understanding that I would be working full-time on the paper and being paid, but when I was given the accounts I found the magazine was deeply in debt. I ended up not being paid and managed to get a job teaching part-time at a further education college in Surrey. When I finished teaching, I would go to the Communist Party HQ in King Street to organise fundraising and edit the paper. Once the debt was paid off, we built circulation from just a few thousand to over 10,000.

During my time in London, I became a member of the editorial board of *Labour Monthly*, a long-standing, widely read and influential journal, initiated in the 1920s by Rajani Palme Dutt, its founding editor, following advice from Lenin. Attending the monthly meetings of the editorial board and listening to the discussion led by Rajani, involving several trade union general secretaries and political figures such as Andrew Rothstein and Robin Page Arnott, was a great education.

After several years in London, and having completed my teacher-training, I returned to Glasgow to work in further education, which I did for the rest of my working life, initially teaching Geology to Surveying students but eventually becoming Vice Principal at Glasgow College of Building and Printing, then Glasgow Metropolitan College (now the City of Glasgow College).

My interest in anti-apartheid, besides my family background and membership of the YCL, stemmed from my time at university where debates were extremely popular in those days. They started at 1.00pm on a Friday and went on continuously until the early hours of Saturday morning. They were run exactly along Westminster lines. A debate was a big event, with around 1,000 people attending. When the pubs shut at 10.00pm, many students flocked to the debates. You had to be entertaining as well as political if you were to hold the crowd. It was a great training ground. I was a member of the Labour Club as at that time there was no Communist Society. Chairs of the Labour Club at Glasgow University usually went onto become MPs, people like John Smith and Donald Dewar, but I didn't want to be that kind of politician.

My maiden speech was in a debate about the sale of arms to the South African apartheid regime. As it was my first speech, I was advised by more senior Labour Club members not to take an intervention on my speech from the Tory front bench, as they were very experienced. But when the time came, I did take an intervention and was asked, 'You are saying a lot about the United Nations' opposition to apartheid, but what do you think about the UN position on Gibraltar?'

Well, I didn't fully understand the issues relating to Gibraltar, so I blustered my way through, describing the Tory intervention as a diversion. However, I went home and read up on Gibraltar and British imperialism. Gibraltar is of strategic importance and so Britain wanted to retain it. The UN had taken the position that it should be returned to Spain – after all, it is really part of Spain. These debates were a good learning experience. More than a decade later, when the Falklands (Malvinas) War was launched by Mrs Thatcher, my understanding of its strategic importance for imperialism, from my reading about Gibraltar those years before, meant that I understood that the Malvinas should be returned to Argentina. I became treasurer of the Committee Against the Falklands War.

Earlier on in my life I was also influenced by people who came to my parents' tenement flat in Temple, near Anniesland in Glasgow, and then later when we moved to Drumchapel. Long before I went to university, I came into contact with people like Cecil Williams, a white South African, who was driving the car that was stopped with Mandela in it when he was arrested and jailed. Mandela spent the next 27 years in prison. Cecil was exiled to the UK and ended up living in Anniesland. My parents became friends of Cecil through their political involvement.

When I was a student, apartheid was a big issue, but remember, this was a time of many anti-capitalist and anti-imperialist struggles, including the 1968 Paris events, the anti-Vietnam war movement and the Upper Clyde Shipbuilders work-in. There was a lot of concern about files being held on student activists and a campaign launched at Warwick University to release these files spread throughout the country. We called a mass meeting and I was elected onto the five-person steering committee. We organised a sit-in of the university offices, including that of the principal. After a few days, the university authorities said we could have access to the files and we ended the sit-in.

At university, I and some others established a Communist Society and we ran a Southern African week. As well as South African speakers, we invited speakers from Angola and Mozambique, where liberation struggles were being fought against Portuguese colonialism. One of the speakers from FRELIMO, Mozambique's liberation movement, arrived on the day his President, Eduardo Mondlane, was assassinated by the Portuguese secret police in 1969. This moved me deeply and I got more and more involved with the liberation struggles in southern Africa.

In 1971, I attended meetings in London where the speaker was Amilcar Cabral, secretary-general of the PAIGC (African Party for the Independence of Guinea and the Cape Verde), which was fighting Portuguese colonialism. Cabral was a most inspiring leader, a freedom fighter and an intellectual. He made a great impression on me. His speeches were published in a pamphlet, *Our People are our Mountains*. He was assassinated in 1973 by the Portuguese.

During my time in London, I met a lot of members of the African National Congress (ANC) who were in exile in Britain, including Yussuf Dadoo and Oliver Tambo. Many later became leaders and government ministers – like Joe Slovo, Aziz Pahad, Essop Pahad and many more. Those three became Ministers in

Mandela's government after the first democratic elections in South Africa in 1994.

The year 1974 saw the defeat of Portuguese fascism and colonialism, as well as the collapse of Spanish fascism and the Greek colonels' regime. I returned to Glasgow in 1974 and was given responsibility by the Glasgow Committee of the Communist Party for solidarity work with Portugal and Spain. This was very welcome, because I got to know all the surviving International Brigadiers, who had fought in the Spanish Civil War in defence of the Republic against Franco's fascists. I became the chair of the Spanish Workers Defence Committee in Scotland and I was very involved in the campaign which created the statue of 'La Pasionaria' on the banks of the River Clyde. The statue is dedicated to the memory of those who fought for the International Brigade against fascism in Spain.

Following the defeat of Portuguese fascism and colonialism, the South Africans invaded Angola but were defeated by a joint Angolan and Cuban military force at the Battle of Cuito Cuanavale – this was decisive in the struggle to liberate southern Africa and showed that the Boers were not invincible.

I attended anti-apartheid meetings at a Quaker's house in Glasgow, only a few people attended, including John Nelson, who was secretary of the group. There were some anti-apartheid groups around Scotland, which came and went sporadically, so we concluded that we should try to coordinate these groups, and an Anti-Apartheid Movement (AAM) Scottish Committee was set up in 1976 with me as chair and John Nelson as secretary. We began to develop more local groups and work with trade unions, churches and local authorities. We coordinated this activity and gave them a lead. John and I continued in these roles until the end of apartheid in 1994 when we became secretary and chair of the successor organisation, Action for Southern Africa (ACTSA) Scotland.

In the 1970s and the 1980s the AAM grew into a mass movement in Britain and became very important in the international solidarity movement. In the 1980s, the AAM played a crucial role when there was a news blackout in South Africa and limited reporting by the mainstream media in Britain. We had to work hard to get information out into the public domain. We used ANC publications as well as our own publications and networks. Mobile phones, the internet, emails and social media did not exist in those days, so we communicated by landline telephones, meetings and post.

I recall one of the exiled South African leaders, M.P. Naicker, editor of *Sechaba*, the ANC journal, asking to speak to me privately and, as we walked down Byres Road in Glasgow, he asked me to assist the underground movement. This got me involved in a number of things, including assisting people with travel documents and recruiting people for various activities. Through my connections, I would get the name of a trusted activist or sympathiser who would be willing to help in some underground activity. I then interviewed them and if appropriate, I would pass them onto the African National Congress. They did not of course know they were being 'interviewed' but this is how we recruited people.

One of those recruits was Stuart Round from Coventry, who I passed on to Mannie Brown of the ANC. A safari company, Africa Hinterland, was set up to take tourists into South Africa in a safari truck. Unbeknown to the tourists – mostly Australians and New Zealanders – under the seats of the truck were specially designed secret compartments housing military arms and explosives destined for the frontline of the ANC's military wing. Stuart drove this truck for a number of years and had several tight escapes from the apartheid regime. A dramatized documentary, *The Secret Safari*, tells the story of this secret mission to smuggle guns into South Africa during the height of apartheid. Following the end of apartheid, Stuart returned to the UK. He had difficulty in securing employment as he had a significant gap in his CV. He applied for a post in the new South African High Commission and asked me to write a reference for him. He got the job and worked for the High Commission for several years.

While all this was happening, our small groups of activists were making a bigger and bigger impact. The Scottish TUC supported our campaign, recognised the ANC and invited representatives of the South African Congress of Trade Unions (SACTU) to their Congresses; we set up 'Scottish Local Authority Action Against Apartheid' of which I became secretary; the churches were heavily involved, as were student unions. We held demonstrations, boycotted shops selling apartheid goods, boycotted Barclays Bank and Shell because of their support for the apartheid regime, picketed the apartheid South Africa Consulate in Glasgow, campaigned for sanctions and generally campaigned for the isolation of apartheid South Africa. We held demonstrations and torchlight processions in many towns and cities in Scotland.

However, it was not just meetings and demonstrations, we also undertook cultural activities. For example, in 1979, we hosted a visit by the cultural group, Mayibuye, and in 1985 we organised a very successful tour of Scotland by Amandla, the ANC's cultural group. They performed to packed audiences at Edinburgh's Assembly Hall during the Festival, Glasgow's Tron Theatre and many other venues in Scotland.

In 1990, the year that Glasgow was designated European City of Culture, we organised the 'Sechaba International Conference and Festival: Cultural Resistance to Apartheid.' We worked very closely with Mendi Msimang, ANC Chief Representative in the UK, and Mongane Wally Serote, ANC Cultural Attaché. The keynote speaker at the conference was Govan Mbeki, one of the

Rivonia trialists along with Mandela, who had recently been released from an apartheid prison after 25 years. Govan's speech was entitled 'Culture in the Struggle for a New South Africa' and was subsequently published in a book, *The End of a Regime? An Anthology of Scottish-South African Writing Against Apartheid*. The book included pieces by Scottish writers such as David Livingstone, Robert Louis Stevenson, Lewis Grassic Gibbon, Hugh MacDiarmid, Naomi Mitchison, Hamish Henderson, Edwin Morgan, Alasdair Gray, Aonghas MacNeacail, Jackie Kay and Jim Kelman; and the South African writers included Sol T. Plaatje, Mazizi Kunene, Alex La Guma, Jeremy Cronin and Mongane Wally Serote.

The opening concert at the Sechaba Festival was the first performance of *I Will Wait* by the Scottish composer, William Sweeney, based on a poem of the same title by the South African Mongane Wally Serote. The piece was performed by the Scottish Chamber Orchestra, the Scottish Philharmonic Singers, the choir of the Association of South African Students and soloist, saxophonist Tommy Smith. The Guest of Honour was Govan Mbeki. It was an electrifying event.

The Sechaba Festival included art, theatre, a comedy night, a writers' evening, a late-night Mandela Club and lots of music, including a week-long Folk Festival with performers including Roy Bailey, Archie Fisher, Rab Noakes and Hamish Imlach.

We also conducted solidarity work with those fighting for the liberation of Zimbabwe and Namibia. I remember chairing a conference in the late 1970s at Strathclyde University, which had speakers from ZAPU and ZANU, the two liberation movements in Rhodesia, as it was at the time. Sam Nujoma, President of the South West Africa People's Organisation (SWAPO) visited and we held large meetings for him in Glasgow and Edinburgh in 1987. During his visit, we hosted a private meeting that brought together trade union, local authority, church and student leaders. Following its liberation from apartheid South Africa Sam Nujoma became the first President of the newly independent Namibia.

Over the years, we built a mass movement against apartheid and in solidarity with the liberation movements of southern Africa.

To create a mass movement, you don't start with masses – you start with an idea and build from there. As Marx said, once an idea grips the masses it becomes a material force. Mass movements can be diverted or lose because of bad leadership so it is important to lead well. Some people today would say that everyone must have been against apartheid as it is now so discredited but that was not the case.

Within the campaign, there were different views on tactics. Some opposed the armed struggle; others were unhappy with Soviet support for the ANC; the Socialist Workers Party (SWP) opposed sanctions – they called them boss's sanctions.

The AAM supported the armed struggle, understanding the reasons for it, as all the peaceful actions against apartheid were met by violence, imprisonment, torture and assassination by the regime. The Soviet Union and the other socialist countries' support for ANC and the other liberation movements was crucial. We had people supporting us, who on other issues such as Ireland had diametrically opposed views, so it was important to keep focused on apartheid. The boycott and sanctions weakened the apartheid regime.

The Anti-Apartheid Movement was a very broad movement indeed. It was not easy to hold it together. No one now confesses to having supported apartheid – even though people did, including the Tories and Prime Minister Margaret Thatcher. Her Ambassador to South Africa during apartheid has even had the temerity to suggest that she was responsible for securing Mandela's release.

When there were setbacks in South Africa, we would see the movement in Britain take a setback; and equally, when there were successes in South Africa, we would get a boost here. The relationship between events there and the ability of the solidarity campaign to respond was very close.

Some people believe we set up the AAM Scottish Committee in 1976 in response to the Soweto uprising that year, but in fact we had been in discussion for some two years beforehand to establish a coordinating committee, draft a constitution, etc. The Soweto uprising saw school students protest against being educated in Afrikaans. It started in Soweto and spread across the country. This was significant as in the 1960s the ANC had been decapitated by the Rivonia Trial with its leaders including Nelson Mandela being imprisoned and many others forced into exile. The struggle had suffered but now there was a new generation of leaders and activists coming to the fore. It gave us a real boost.

Looking back, it is interesting to reflect on the twists, turns and events that affected what we were doing. At one point in 1979, the Lord Provost of Glasgow, David Hodge, hosted the South African ambassador for lunch in the City Chambers. We held a picket of the event. One thousand people turned out to protest. David Hodge did not recant and was expelled from the Labour Group but remained as Lord Provost until the following election. In an interview at the time he said, 'You can't expect people to come out of the jungle and go straight into government!' This was an allusion to events in Rhodesia at that time which, when liberated, became Zimbabwe. There was a huge furore about these comments.

In the aftermath, a resolution was passed at Kelvingrove Labour Party calling for Nelson Mandela to be given the Freedom of the City. The resolution went through various committees, including the Glasgow District Committee of the Labour Party and the Labour Group, and was eventually adopted by the council. Nelson Mandela received the Freedom of the City of Glasgow on 4 August 1981, when he was still incarcerated on Robben Island. Glasgow was the first city in the world to confer this honour on Mandela. The Tory Group on the council boycotted the event.

At the ceremony, I spent some time unsuccessfully trying to persuade officials that Ruth Mompati, ANC Chief Representative in the UK, should be on the platform. The Vice President of Nigeria, Dr Alex Ekwueme, accepted the award on Mandela's behalf. This was good, as it gave a high profile to the ceremony, but the reluctance to have the ANC recognised was probably due to caution about supporting the armed struggle. Mandela was still seen by some as a terrorist. The media used this to denounce the award.

At the lunch following the formal ceremony, the Vice President of Nigeria gave a speech and invited people to attend the Anti-Apartheid Movement meeting later that afternoon. The meeting was held in one of the Committee rooms in the City Chambers. I chaired the meeting with Ruth Mompati outlining the struggle of the South African people and Vice-President Ekwueme explaining why Nigeria had nationalised British Petroleum for busting UN sanctions against Rhodesia.

That evening the Vice President hosted a banquet for a large gathering and Ruth and I were invited to sit at the top table.

The bestowal of the Freedom of the City got huge attention. High Commissioners from 16 Commonwealth countries attended the ceremony. Mike Terry, AAM Executive Secretary, and I developed an idea that through E.S. Reddy of the UN Special Committee Against Apartheid we would get Lord Provost Michael Kelly invited to the UN in New York to launch a campaign to get mayors from around the world to support the call for Mandela's release and the end of apartheid, and to encourage other cities to follow Glasgow's lead and grant him Freedom of the City status. The UN Special Committee invited Michael Kelly to New York to launch the petition and several thousand mayors signed it, calling for Mandela's release. Michael was a good PR person and was ideal for the role – we were on a roll and support for the cause was gaining momentum.

In 1984 Aberdeen City Council awarded the Freedom of the City to Nelson and Winnie Mandela by 30 votes to 13. The opposition was led by the Tories, whose council leader commented, 'The obvious conclusion is that any political rabble-rouser who is sympathetic to the socialist cause could be in for becoming a Freeman of Aberdeen.' For several years thereafter, Aberdeen AAM group held a demonstration to celebrate the award.

We established the Scottish Committee for Local Authority Action Against Apartheid in 1985 and I was appointed secretary. The committee coordinated the actions of local authorities throughout Scotland, particularly during the annual ten days of action throughout Britain from 16 June (anniversary of the Soweto Uprising) until 26 June (anniversary of the signing of the Freedom Charter). Local authorities held meetings, renamed streets and buildings, publicised the boycott and flew the flag of the African National Congress.

On 12 June 1985, the 21st anniversary of the life-sentencing of Nelson Mandela and the other Rivonia trialists, we organised for the next Lord Provost of Glasgow, Bob Gray, to lead a delegation of lord provosts, lord mayors and mayors calling for Mandela's release to 10 Downing Street, where Mrs Thatcher was the incumbent. She remained unmoved.

In 1986 Dundee conferred the Freedom of the City on Nelson Mandela. That same year, Edinburgh District Council unveiled a statue named 'Woman and Child' in Festival Square, dedicated to the freedom fighters of the South African liberation movement. It had never been possible for the Labour Group to find the necessary two-thirds majority on the council to award the Freedom of Edinburgh to Mandela. Edinburgh did make the award in 1998 some years after the end of apartheid when Mandela visited the city to attend the Commonwealth Heads of Government Meeting.

In addition to the three Scottish cities which conferred Freedom of the City awards on Mandela, Midlothian District Council, as one of its many anti-apartheid activities over the years, also conferred the award.

Four authorities in England (Newcastle, Hull, Sheffield and the London Borough of Greenwich) and one in Wales (Islwyn) also conferred the award.

The idea to rename a street in Glasgow was mooted. Some people thought it should be George Square, as it was Glasgow's main square. I disagreed as I believed renaming George Square might lose us support. In the end, it was agreed to rename St George's Place, where the Apartheid South African Consulate was located on the fifth floor of the Stock Exchange Building, which we regularly picketed. It was also appropriate as it symbolised the support for apartheid by big business. The street was renamed Nelson Mandela Place.

This resulted in a media frenzy. The South Africans hated it and refused to use the address and instead used a Post Office Box, but every time they looked out of their windows they couldn't avoid seeing Mandela's name.

In 1985/86, the apartheid regime declared a State of Emergency and there was a general news blackout. As a consequence, the BBC stopped reporting events in South Africa. Mass arrests were made under the Pass Laws, with 400,000 arrested in 1986 alone. We arranged a picket of the apartheid consulate every Friday for over a year and got shop stewards, students and activists on a rota to picket. We would have 60 or 70 people every Friday keeping the issue in the public domain.

Within the ANC there were some difficulties and differences of opinion on tactics. Some saw the elevation of Mandela at the expense of other political prisoners and of the more general struggle as a problem. They did not want to see the cult of the personality emerge around one man. There was also concern that, from prison, he might be engaging in dialogue with the regime. However, that was resolved and the slogan became, 'Release Mandela and all political prisoners.'

In 1988, the first London Wembley Mandela music concert was held and the following day we sent off 25 marchers (one for every year he had been in prison at that point) to London. There was a demonstration of some 30,000 from Kelvingrove via Nelson Mandela Place to a huge rally in Glasgow Green. Oliver Tambo, the ANC Acting President, was the main speaker at the event, which I chaired. Other speakers at the rally included Reverend Allan Boesak of the United Democratic Front, Campbell Christie of the STUC and SWAPO leader, Andimba Toivo ja Toivo.

In a conversation with Oliver Tambo prior to the rally, he was frank with me and said there were tensions within the ANC and the regime were exploiting this. The South African intelligence service, the Bureau of State Security (BOSS) was very active with agents here. They bombed the ANC office in London and conducted other activities to disrupt the Anti-Apartheid Movement.

We were constantly under surveillance by both the South Africans (BOSS) and the British (Special Branch) at the time. I was often followed, and I discovered that my family home was under surveillance. My telephone was also tapped. I knew this as the tap clearly wasn't always working properly – at one point when I tried to make phone calls it kept putting me directly through to Partick Marine Police Station, where Special Branch was located.

The confidential police files were obtained... following freedom of information requests. Leading Scots figures on file included the late Jim Knapp, former leader of the National Union of Railwaymen, and Brian Filling, chair of the Scottish Anti-Apartheid Movement.

By the late 1980s in South Africa, trade unions had become mass organisations taking effective action and the Congress of South African Trade Unions (COSATU) had been created; the United Democratic Front had been formed involving thousands of people and hundreds of organisations; sanctions were biting hard. The white settler regime in Rhodesia and the Portuguese colonies of Angola, Guinea Bissau and Mozambique had all fallen. The apartheid regime was in deep trouble. Its western supporters were left with the dilemma of whether to keep Mandela in jail as a martyr and symbol of resistance or to release him.

The Mandela Wembley concert had raised the profile of the anti-apartheid struggle across the world and in South Africa the country was becoming ungovernable. There was economic and social chaos. Pressure was huge. On 11 February 1990, Mandela was released and we called a celebratory gathering in Nelson Mandela Place that evening. Hundreds of people attended, bringing the traffic to a standstill. Other celebrations were held in Edinburgh and elsewhere.

Between Mandela's release and the first free, democratic elections in April 1994, some 10,000 people were killed in what the mainstream media referred to as 'black on black' violence. However, the reality was that there was a 'Third Force' at work, promoted by the apartheid security services to undermine the African National Congress and create divisions. The regime targeted the hostels where many migrant workers from the so-called Bantustans lived. The residents were given alcohol and guns and encouraged into violence against the people in the townships. Negotiations were under way between the ANC and De Klerk regime, but no election date had been agreed. On Easter weekend 1993, Chris Hani, general secretary of the South African Communist Party and a very popular ANC leader, was assassinated. There was a huge outpouring of grief and anger at this act and an enormous mobilisation of the people by ANC in protest. It wasn't De Klerk who went on television but Mandela to plead for calm. The apartheid regime negotiators were pressurised into finally agreeing an election date. The balance of power had shifted.

Local Authority Action Against Apartheid invited Nelson Mandela to the UK to receive the Freedoms of the nine UK cities which had made the award. I was appointed to liaise with Mandela's office, the ANC and the nine local authorities, to organise the visit. Mandela's office and the ANC were easy to deal with as they wanted the event to be held in one place given Mandela's age and it was in the run-up to the historic election. However, understandably, all the UK local authorities wanted him to come to their town or city. It took almost two years of negotiation to achieve agreement that the event would be held in one place.

Nelson Mandela arrived in Glasgow on Friday 8 October 1993 and collected the Freedoms of the nine UK cities at a special ceremony in Glasgow City Chambers on Saturday 9 October 1993. He met ten delegates from each city, town and borough separately and then addressed a gathering of some 400 people in the banqueting hall of the City Chambers. Afterwards, he addressed a huge rally in George Square, which I chaired. In his speech, Mandela raised the issue of the 'Third Force' proxy murders by the regime. It was a very difficult four years from Mandela's release until the election in 1994. The rally ended in George Square with him dancing with Marah Louw, the South African singer, to the delight of the rain-swept crowd. On the Sunday, we held a press conference very early in the morning for newspaper editors, as Mandela was flying to Ireland at lunchtime. The editors were rather unhappy with the timing of the press conference; however, they did attend. Mandela started the proceedings by saying that rather than make a speech he would begin by answering the questions that were already prominent in the media, 'What was his personal relationship with Winnie and what was his political relationship with Chief Buthelezi?' Having answered these questions candidly, he went on to talk about the apartheid regime's 'Third Force' causing murder and mayhem designed to divide the majority and derail election process. The editors were enthralled by Mandela and gave him a standing ovation. This resulted in positive and widespread media coverage. As Mandela spent the whole weekend in Glasgow and as I was staying in the same hotel and was the lead organiser of the events, I was fortunate to spend a lot of time with him.

When the election was held on 27 April 1994 in South Africa, it was a fantastic day, with snaking crowds queuing for hours for their first democratic vote. Mandela was voting for the first time, at the age of 76. It was a hugely emotional moment. Following the election, I was very privileged to be invited as a guest to attend Nelson Mandela's inauguration as President of the Republic of South Africa on 10 May 1994 in Pretoria.

At the ceremony in union buildings, I sat beside Dennis Goldberg, one of the Rivonia trialists, who had spent 22 years in Pretoria Central Prison. On his release from prison in 1985, Denis had come to the UK and I had organised a speaking tour for him in Scotland. Over the succeeding years, we worked closely together and became good friends. Denis and I were at the ceremony very early and we met people who were coming together for the first time in decades, many only recently out of exile or prison. It was a joyous and emotional occasion.

In December 1994, I led a 33-strong Scottish delegation to the new South Africa. Aziz Pahad, deputy foreign minister, hosted a lunch for the delegation in the South African Parliament on the day of our arrival. Thabo Mbeki, deputy president, met a group of us privately and then we accompanied him to the chamber for President's Question Time. Thabo was taking this as acting president while Nelson Mandela was out of the country. One of the questions put to him by a Nationalist MP was, 'How many illegal immigrants are in the country?' Mbeki replied, 'From which year do you wish us to start counting illegal immigrants?' His response met with laughter and much applause as it was taken as a reference to the early colonialists.

During our visit to Parliament, we had meetings with many other ANC leaders, including Cyril Ramaphosa, who had led the negotiations on behalf of ANC and was chair of the Constitutional Assembly at that time. He is now president of the country.

Ronnie Kasrils, the new deputy defence minister, hosted us in Cape Town barracks. The colonel who gave us a guided tour talked about his military service in the frontline states of Angola, Mozambique and Namibia. These were the countries where the so-called 'South African Defence Force' was deployed to attack ANC, SWAPO and the other liberation movements. This was the colonel's recent history and you could feel the tension between the old white military establishment and the new ANC government led by a man they had jailed for decades as a terrorist. Given the situation and the balance of forces, not least the military, it was understandable that Mandela sought reconciliation.

The new government set up the Reconstruction and Development Programme (RDP) led by a cabinet minister, Jay Naidoo, formerly general secretary of the Congress of South African Trade Unions (COSATU). Within two years, it had given way to a new programme entitled the Growth, Employment and Reconstruction (GEAR) Plan, under pressure from the international business community. This move led towards a more business friendly, pro-capital focus. It was of course at a time of a new world order with the defeat of the Soviet Union and the dominance of capital internationally.

The accession to power of the ANC gave rise to those who saw it as a vehicle for personal advancement. In 1997, only three years after the end of apartheid, Nelson Mandela in his Presidential Political Report to the 50th National Conference of ANC, stated:

In reality, during the last three years, we have found it difficult to deal with such careerists in a decisive manner. We, ourselves, have therefore allowed the space to emerge for these opportunists to pursue their counter-revolutionary goals, to the detriment of our movement and struggle. During this period, we have also been faced with various instances of corruption involving our own members, including those who occupy positions of authority by virtue of the victory of the democratic revolution...

Notwithstanding Mandela's warning, these problems of opportunism, careerism and corruption continued.

In addition, there was the introduction of the Black Economic Empowerment (BEE) programme, later retitled the Broad-Based Black Economic Empowerment (BBEE) programme. This programme created a black middle class. Corruption became a very serious problem, particularly under the Zuma presidency. He has been charged and is now on trial. There are those in the ANC who are determined to deal with corruption but there are many in positions of power and influence who will resist this.

If I reflect on what we did in the anti-apartheid struggle, there are many lessons. If you want to build a movement, you need a vision of where you are going and what your ultimate aim is. Your enemies will try to stop, divide and divert you. They will use agents and encourage opportunists. All of that is inevitable. You need to hold to your vision. You need to understand the forces at play and the power of unity and the importance of it. This is often underestimated. To hold unity on a principled basis is very important.

One of the lessons I learned from South Africans was about unity and differences. In African culture, people have differences, but they will find a way of talking to each other again. With that approach, you can keep people with differences together for the greater goal.

Another lesson is to be realistic, acknowledge when things are not going well, and if necessary, change your strategy or tactics, not your aim. People often said to me, 'You must have thought about giving up! You must have asked yourself if you would see the end of apartheid or see socialism in your lifetime.' But I don't think like that, I don't get negative or pessimistic. I knew the opponents of South African liberation were powerful and wealthy, as are the opponents of socialism and would not give up their power and privilege easily. There is no reason to be pessimistic if you are clear about the justice of your case and work hard and intelligently to win support for your goal.

There are examples from history where we have won, and new generations will learn from those struggles, as well as those we have lost. Sometimes these are hard lessons. In the end, I believe the mass of the people will see and understand who is right and who is wrong. In the struggle to end Apartheid that is what happened. No matter how much the establishment, big business interests and the mainstream media were against us, ours became a mass movement across the world. Symbolic actions like granting the Freedom of the City, which in practice may not seem to mean a lot, took on a great importance, resonated and mobilised a lot of people. Sometimes acts like that catch the imagination of masses of people, move them into action, expose and isolate the minority who hold power.

The anti-apartheid struggle of the South African people led by the African National Congress and supported by the international solidarity movement showed that victory is possible.

MARIA FYFE

A One-Woman Show

Maria Fyfe (who died at the age of 82 in December 2020) was a fiercely proud Glaswegian who fought for women's rights and battled sexism within the workplace.

During her political life, she stood up against some of the dinosaurs in Glasgow's council chambers and in Westminster, never allowing herself to be silenced or to see the issues she cared about sidelined. She drove many of the changes in employment practices in Glasgow City Council, challenging discrimination in all forms.

The only woman among the 50 Scottish Labour MPs elected to the UK Parliament in 1987, Maria represented Maryhill until 2001. She was at the forefront of campaigns for equal pay, fair employment practices, tampon safety, fair council funding and women's reproductive health.

Following her retirement, she was at the heart of the campaign to erect a statue to social justice campaigner and Red Clydesider, Mary Barbour, in Govan.

I WAS BORN in Glasgow in 1938. My family lived in a tenement in the Gorbals until we moved to Govanhill when I was four. We were moving up in the world – we had electric lighting instead of gas and our own indoor toilet instead of sharing one on the stair.

I went to Holy Cross Primary School. In fact, I went to many primary schools because my family moved around a lot; onwards and upwards, as they say.

We moved from Govanhill to Knightswood for a brief period and then my mother and father had a stroke of good luck getting one of the early council houses built in Pollok after the war. I remember my parents saying this was where they would settle for good. It was a terrace of houses with front and back gardens. There were no side roads, just muddy tracks; when it came to my first holy communion, my older brother by eight years, Joe, carried me along the muddy pathway to the road where the church stood so I wouldn't get my long white dress dirty.

I went to Notre Dame High School, having done well in 'the Quali' as they called it then. My elder brother by ten years, Jim, was at university after he was demobbed from the RAF and got to know women students who had been at Notre Dame. He saw what an advantage that had been for them, it got them into university; it was expected if you went to Notre Dame. He had told my mother about it and urged her to apply for me.

I was not politically aware at that age. I just felt, *Oh gosh, I'm going to be going to a school just like in the stories*, not only wearing a box-pleated gymslip but a tie and a panama hat. The uniform was a ridiculous expense for families.

My dad worked as a tram driver. He was very influential in my political development. He was the eldest of five and very clever at school. So much so, that his class teacher in the final primary year spoke to his parents and urged them to let him go to Saint Aloysius, the top Catholic private school in Glasgow. He was so keen that my dad should go there that he said he would pay for his books for as long as he stayed but my parents turned the offer down. They said he needed to get out to work as soon as possible to contribute to the family income. It was not just a case of working-class poverty; my grandfather drank a bucket of whisky and that had an impact on my dad's life. It also made him a lifelong tee teetotaller.

In his work, he took up issues with the management. He was an active trade unionist in the Transport and General Workers' Union and, particularly interesting for that period, he took up the cause of the conductresses who were on the staff where he worked in Langside depot. I am not sure what position he held within the union, if any, but they looked to him as the person who would talk to the management on their behalf. He raised issues such as when the women wanted to wear trousers in the winter and not be forced to wear skirts. Dad put it to the management that on those open-ended trams in cold weather night and day, it was only sensible to let the women wear trousers if they wished and it would cut down sickness absence too. The management agreed to this sensible request.

I liked that he would speak up for people and get things done. That impressed me. I had also been impressed by the story of my grandfather, the same grandfather who was too fond of the drink. The family story was that he was a member of the Knights of St Columba and some wealthy local grocer had offered to give £5 for a raffle prize. My grandfather apparently said at the meeting, 'We cannot accept this money until he pays his staff decent wages.' I liked that. Apparently, this row broke up the branch – when I heard that story I wanted to be like my grandad.

So, my father and grandfather were influential but not politically active in the formal sense. My dad always voted Labour but was never active in the party and my mother was so apolitical that when I joined the Young Socialists she actually said to me, 'Why don't you join the Young Conservatives, you are more likely to meet a young man with a well-paid job there.' I said, 'Mum, I want to beat the Conservatives, not join them!'

In spite of my successful beginning, I didn't actually do that well at school. I was bored with the subjects. I kept reading other stuff that had nothing to do with school. I did better at languages than anything else and was utterly hopeless at science, but I didn't fancy doing a languages degree. I wasn't even aware there were subjects like Economics, Sociology and suchlike, so I went to commercial college and qualified in business studies – well, to an extent, as I left it before the three years were up because I didn't want to teach shorthand and typing. My first job was secretary to the editor of *Scottish Field* magazine.

I knew nothing whatsoever about field sports, but all the editor cared about was my shorthand and typing speeds. He had been a court reporter himself and he took fantastically fast shorthand notes, but my speed was good enough to keep up with him dictating notes, as they did then. It seems like another world now, doesn't it?

I worked at that for a wee while and was actually trying to get into journalism, but in those days, it was hopeless for women, outside cookery and fashion. So, what to do then?

I ended up working with the Gas Board. I was secretary to three bosses at first. Then I was promoted to work for a higher-level boss and that was when I took up my first battle.

I discovered that all of the secretarial staff were paid less than the clerical staff and I thought: this is wrong, because you can't get a secretarial job at any level without taking training in shorthand and typing and other secretarial skills at your own expense, yet we're paid less than people who have come straight out of school and done nothing extra. It was not fair, so I took it up in the union first of all. Our male members said, 'Och, it's us that compose the letters, all you do is type them up.' I wasn't having that and got a meeting of the women together and said, 'Even our own union isn't listening to us and the management certainly will not listen if the union doesn't. Why don't we for one day type exactly what is dictated to us, with all the umms and errs and bits that should be left out, kept in. If he coughs type caa caa caa and don't correct grammar.' We chortled to ourselves as we carried out our plan. We were not on strike. We were doing exactly what we were told. That happened for one day and the management said, 'Ok, we'll discuss this with the union, but we've got to do it through the whole of the Scottish system and we will set up a working party to decide which job is equivalent to which.'

Here is the annoying bit. By the time this happened I was engaged to Jim Fyfe. He was working as a railway clerk and our plan was that he should go to university at the newly opened Strathclyde campus and get a degree first, then I would go later. However, the wife of a student who received the married student grant could not do full-time work, so I had to leave. That was the rule then, so I never saw the benefit of the change in pay that we had won.

Another thing that got me at the time was quite interesting because now it would be illegal. When we were looking for a house to rent we found out the Gas Board held some properties and I found there was a nice little cottage available close to the gas holder near where I now live. However, I was told women staff couldn't have that – why not? Because women staff leave and have babies. I said, 'First, not all women do leave and have babies – and even if they do sometimes, they come back to work. Second, men also leave their jobs for career moves, but that does not stop them from getting a house. It's not fair.' Nothing ever came of that one, but that's what made me a feminist as well as a socialist, thinking these are the kind of things that are unfair and must be put right.

I went to university after Jim qualified. I took Social Studies, including Economic History and English. That was what I ended up doing my honours degree in. I just loved every minute of that course, it was fantastic. It chimed so much with my politics. Working-class history was right up my street. I never have been much interested in kings and queens.

After graduation, I went to teacher-training college for a year, but I did not actually work in schools because a vacancy arose in Falkirk Technical College to teach General Studies there. The pay was better and it was closer to home than the nearest available school, so I did that for a couple of years.

Then came a great move for me. My brother Joe noticed an advert in *The*

Herald. It said that there was going to be a Trade Union Studies unit set up in Central College in the middle of Glasgow and they were looking for staff who had industrial relations experience and a social sciences degree. I applied, thinking, 'I have no heavy industry experience, but I do have office experience and have been active in NALGO. At Falkirk Tech I was a rep for the Educational Institute of Scotland (EIS) and had won a campaign there.

Falkirk Council wanted to stop the General Studies staff teaching higher subjects and confine them to non-certificated subjects. We enjoyed our work with the craft students, but we didn't only want to do that. We wanted to keep up with our specialist subjects and we had a good record of success with students who, for one reason or another, had not done well when at school. My colleagues and I took a lot of pleasure in teaching people whose school days had not been successful, and then found they could grasp what they had not been able to grasp before. On behalf of the EIS branch, I wrote to the Director of Education and chair of the Education Committee, highlighting the enjoyment of our work and how we were helping adults who were seizing a second chance achieving their Highers and moving into new careers or higher education. The council changed their minds and let us continue. I referred to that story when I applied for the Trade Union Studies lecturing post – a job I loved and continued until I was elected to Parliament (I did it part-time when I was a councillor).

In 1959, Labour had lost three general elections in a row and a new book called *Must Labour Lose?* was getting a lot of attention. It was the first political book I ever read and it horrified me. I said to myself, we cannot allow this, it just should not happen. The Labour Party that had created a brand new home for my family and had created the National Health Service could not just be written off. I felt we had to do something.

My brother Joe said we could always see if we can help. So, I rounded up some pals and we went along to the Labour Rooms in Craigton and knocked the door and asked if we could help. We were welcomed in. Then the Young Socialists were started up, the former League of Youth having been disbanded because of Trotskyist influence in earlier years. For years I was an activist, not seeking any senior involvement until many years later.

Jean McFadden was Leader of the Labour Group on a hung council in Glasgow, where the SNP held the balance of power and kept changing their minds about what they wanted. At our branch meeting, one night early in 1980, Jean said we need some new candidates and we would work with them to win power. She urged people to step forward, so I did and decided to go for it. I did not immediately succeed. At one branch selection meeting, they asked, 'How will you look after your children, if elected?' I replied, 'I expect you are asking the male candidates the same question?' I don't think they liked that. That institutional sexism existed in all political parties then, it was rife in society. However, I was selected and had a great relationship with the local party and the community right up until I entered Parliament.

There were two distinct political groupings within the ruling Labour Group at that time. Jean McFadden was keen to promote an equalities agenda and I started to call on the council to provide a nursery for staff and the children of councillors. Pat Lally, who led the other grouping, was opposed. He said ratepayers would not accept it. I won a commitment for this in the budget one year but there were then manoeuvres to ensure the cash went unspent. Pat was also opposed to setting up a Women's Committee. I then suggested an equal opportunities subcommittee of the personnel committee, of which I was convener. This was difficult for opponents to resist.

We introduced some things that are now old hat. For example, we ended the practice of putting the name of a person's school on job applications to try and break down discrimination on religious grounds. We advertised jobs making it crystal clear they were open to anyone irrespective of gender, religion, race, etc. We created an equal pay scheme for manual workers. We pushed through a progressive agenda.

I was on the council for seven years. It was a politically satisfying period. I spent four years as deputy city treasurer to Bob Gray, always looking at how we could spend the money we had in the best way and to defend communities against Thatcher's attacks. Some left-wingers had a strange attitude, saying no one on the left should do the finance role. Why did they think it should be left to right-wingers to manage the money?

These were tough times too. Labour councils who wanted to put up a stronger resistance to the Tories got together and we worked with Stirling, Sheffield, the GLC, etc, trying to organise a fight-back. Only three members of the council wanted to follow the militant line in Liverpool, the rest of us rejected that approach. Their line of 'no rent rises, no rate rises, no cuts' really irritated me. How were we going to pay for services and keep people in jobs with that approach? What would we do when the money ran out because the government was cutting our grant by such a huge amount?

To cover my selection and election to Parliament, I need to go back a little. In about 1970, Jim and I, with our two boys, moved to Cumbernauld. We got fed up with the Labour Party at that time and were frustrated at the party's failure to address the issue of devolution. I made the greatest mistake of my life at this time, when I joined Jim Sillars' new Scottish Labour Party. I had no idea that Jim Sillars was such a dictator; all I heard was his great speeches and oratory. I learned a hard lesson not to be lured by fine rhetoric. If you disagreed with Jim on anything, you were accused of being a 'Trot infiltrator'. The party was doomed. Two branches were in dispute with Sillars over the EU and he decided to expel them over the heads of the entire membership. At the conference I went to the rostrum to oppose this and said, 'By all means expel individuals who are causing harm, but not entire branches.' That was unfair. In response, he closed down our branch too!

Now, I am not a person who cries a lot, but I went home in tears that day. It made it all the more annoying that on the radio at home that night, Donald Dewar was doing his Radio Clyde politics show and was enjoying the spectacle of the chaos in Sillars' party. Donald and I laughed about it years later.

Before we returned to Glasgow in the mid-'70s, the Labour Party in Cumbernauld wanted Janey Buchan as the parliamentary candidate. Even the right of the party liked her and supported her, but the Transport and General Workers' Union wanted one of their own in the seat and packed out the selection meeting for one of their conveners in the car industry down south (he went on to win the selection but lost the actual election to the Tories in a year when Labour had done pretty well). We should have won that seat.

I vividly recall, in the snow of that year, I was standing at a polling station and saw a man being brought in on a stretcher, he was so determined to cast his vote.

Back in Glasgow, as a member of the council, I had been on a deputation to the House of Commons protesting about the huge cuts to Glasgow's budget. We had a meeting with Michael Foot, who was very sympathetic. I hadn't visited Parliament before, so I was sitting in the gallery and watched all these Tories who hadn't been anywhere near the debate coming in, dinner-jacketed and bow-tied, to vote through the cuts to my city. I was furious about this and thought, 'I want to be an MP and stick up for Glasgow.' Prior to that, I thought, 'Well if Janey Buchan can't make it, what hope have I?'

However, it was fortuitous I hadn't tried for any other seat because I had agreed to Jimmy Allison's request (he was then Scottish organiser for the Labour Party) that I should go for a hopeless seat to gain experience. But that hadn't yet been arranged. Then, Jim Craigen, the sitting MP for Maryhill, a seat that had recently been created from the existing Maryhill constituency and a sizeable section from Kelvingrove, decided he wanted to go and work in the housing movement. He had listened to some of his more hysterical colleagues believing he would be deselected, but that was never on the cards for him in Maryhill as he had support from his old Maryhill base and most of the left would have given him time to build up relations with the local party. Working-class people are reluctant to sack people unless something very serious is wrong, so I think he totally misread the situation.

A shortlist of five candidates was drawn up. I expected Danny Crawford, a local councillor born and bred in the area with good links to the local people, to win. Another candidate was a Trotskyist woman from Aberdeen, who said she thought the Labour Party was racist. I remember getting angry about this, saying, 'Like any big organisation there will be racists in it, but let me say this: if I thought the Labour Party was racist, I wouldn't be a member of it.' There was also a Co-operative Party candidate. Jim Craigen had been a Labour and Co-op candidate, so they thought they should secure the selection again. A further candidate was Jim McKechnie, an old friend of mine from the SLP days and a Strathclyde regional councillor. He and I made a pact to ask each other's supporters to transfer their votes to the other should one of us drop out in the exhaustive ballot. After the voting was finished, I was surprised and delighted to be selected in what then was a very safe seat. The *Evening Times* editorial reported that a 'Glasgow housewife' had been picked to fight the seat for Labour. Someone I didn't know wrote in, tearing strips off them for this comment.

The public did not seem to mind, as I won by over 19,000, doubling the Labour majority. I was the only woman in a Labour Group of 50.

This made me realise I was going to have to take up loads of issues that were mainly of concern to women, as well as regarding every issue as a women's issue. More women would have spread the load. Not that I minded, far from it. I was delighted to be made Jo Richardson's deputy, and I did get support from some of my male colleagues. It wasn't their fault that the media phoned me for a comment whenever the story was about a woman being sexually assaulted or living with domestic violence. Why did they never think of asking a male colleague what they thought of a child molester being let off, or equal pay being still a distant dream, or women being cajoled by their husband or partner to have an operation to increase the size of her breasts? When the latter topic was raised with me, I said women should reply: 'How about getting your beer belly reduced first and see how that goes?' My colleague Sam Galbraith laughed, saying that was the perfect answer.

I think of myself as quite an amiable person, but in Parliament I got to know how 'ithers saw me'. I've been called 'intimidating' and 'terrifying' by journalists, and that really puzzles me. Maybe because of representing Maryhill, the place of the TV cop *Taggart* fame, one member actually asked me how did a woman become MP for a tough place like that? Or is it just that I speak bluntly and don't plead?

Once when I posed a question to the 'semi-house-trained polecat' Norman Tebbit, John Home Robertson asked me, 'Are you not afraid of anybody?' Well, of course not. Those were days when women MPs were barracked but never had any reason to fear assault or murder. Vicious tweets did not exist. Now these vicious attacks and the murder of Jo Cox are an assault on the very idea of parliamentary democracy. Women fought so long for the right to vote and be elected to Parliament, and I never thought I'd see the day when we'd have to defend parliamentary democracy against right-wing populists. But fight back we must.

The Labour Group of Scottish MPs was divided into two groups, one disparagingly known as 'the Jimmies', the other as the 'Annabelle's set', after the London nightclub of the same name. I was advised by someone I was seen as a member of the latter, despite never having set foot in the place in my life. I think it is fair to say that the working-class MPs who hadn't been to university felt they were looked down upon by some who were highly qualified, and they were right. Some did. I fell between two stools, as I was working-class but had gone on to higher education as a mature student.

That year, there was a big increase in the number of Labour women MPs elected: 41, up from 23. We worked together on many issues. Jo Richardson was a strong feminist and she became my mentor. She travelled around the country as shadow minister for women, speaking to women's groups. I became her deputy. When New Labour came along, I was very angry with Peter Mandelson, who prevented Jo from speaking at events or appearing on platforms. She didn't seem to fit in with his image of a shiny New Labour Party.

The earliest campaign I got involved in was the anti-blacklisting campaign. I had seen a *World in Action* documentary on the issue and learned that one of my constituents who was involved in the Anti-Apartheid Movement had been blacklisted. Then one day soon after, I was asked by Clare Short to stand in the queue until she could get there, to try and get a slot for a ten-minute rule bill debate. A whip came to tell me, 'Clare can't make it, you can take her slot.' So, I took my chance and did a ten-minute rule bill on blacklisting. It failed, because the large Tory majority all opposed it. I then established the Anti-Blacklisting Campaign which was supported by senior people like John Smith, David Blunkett and many from other parties, including Ian Paisley. But not a single Tory.

When one of the key players in the blacklisting operation fell out with them, he handed their list to us, so we gave it to the *Daily Mirror* and the *Daily Record* who lapped it up and published stories for days. In '97 Labour brought in legislation against blacklisting and we thought that was it. The Economic League was struggling and eventually folded. Some senior politicians thought there was no need to kill something already dead, so they didn't put the legislation before the Queen for her signature, it hadn't received royal assent, and there we were thinking it was all done and dusted. Unbelievable.

When I became deputy to Jo we did a lot of work on issues affecting women, especially on toxic shock syndrome caused by an overgrowth of bacteria in women using highly absorbent tampons, which can cause avoidable deaths. I brought forward another ten-minute rule bill on tampon safety and when it was being introduced I got letters telling me I shouldn't be wasting time on such nonsense.

On the day my bill came before Parliament, the clerk was about to read out the name of my bill. Tory Nicholas Soames was sitting near me and asked what was my bill all about? So, I said to him, 'Wait and see.' Then the clerk shouted out, 'THE TAMPON SAFETY BILL!' and Soames slumped in his seat and said audibly, 'What is this place coming to?'

In the end, the government took it up and we got agreement from the tampon manufacturers to provide much more advice to women, so they would avoid health problems while using this essential product, and they would know that if they did experience illness to get to A&E as fast as possible.

I had been convinced for years that Scotland needed a range of legislative powers, while remaining in the UK. Even when we had a Labour government, the needs of Scottish councils could be ignored by Whitehall. True, Yorkshire and Lancashire had the same complaint, but Scotland was a different case, because we had separate systems of law, education and local government.

So, when voices were raised demanding a Scottish Parliament I heartily joined in, but with one difference that had not arisen in the past. I told my party colleagues I would not be interested if this was going to be another case of jobs for the boys. In the Scottish Constitutional Convention, I chaired an equalities working party looking at issues such as working hours and crèche provision, as well as how to achieve 50/50 representation throughout, not just in the Labour ranks. That did not succeed, but we did reach a percentage that put us up there alongside the Scandinavian countries.

I took part in the STUC Women's Committee 50/50 campaign. Eventually, after many a dust-up at our party conferences, we won the argument and the Scottish Parliament began its work with equal numbers of Labour men and women MSPs. I had also pursued in Parliament the idea of legal enforcement for all parties to secure equal representation, which had been found doable by the French Parliament, but got a no-no from the Labour leadership.

I was often asked why I did not seek election to the Scottish Parliament myself. The reason was simply that Westminster was to retain policy areas in which I had greatest interest, such as international affairs, aid to developing countries and macro-economic issues.

I never thought we would be where we are now, with endless debate about a second referendum on independence. The Indy vote has gone up, provoked by Boris Johnson. But he won't be there for ever.

By 2001, I was into my 60s and thought I would like to retire before I reached 65. I was also unwell with a long post-viral illness. The next election was coming and I felt I would not be able to campaign as I would like to. I thought it was the right time to go. No one pressured me to do it. I told no one that I was worried about my health. You are not allowed to be ill if you are an MP, you know.

However, I did not give up on politics when I retired. One of the things I got involved in was a socialist women's choir. One of their songs was 'Mrs Barbour's Army.' You could get the impression from the song that Mary Barbour had risen from obscurity, ran an amazingly successful campaign against rising rents and landlordism during the early 1900s and then disappeared again. I thought this very unlikely, so I started researching her and found that she was an amazing woman who was in the Independent Labour Party, organised a women's housing association along with Helen Crawfurd and Agnes Dolan, campaigned against slum housing and, in 1915, led a fantastic campaign that forced the government to put rents back down to pre-war levels. These were women who did not have the vote.

It had puzzled me that you could read any number of accounts of Red Clydeside and the heroes of that time with no mention of any women. I recall discussing this with some of my female comrades and we asked ourselves why women were not taking part. Was it because they had strenuous domestic duties then compared to now? Were they looking after children while the men went to the meetings? Or were there other reasons? The reality is we never even knew they had existed, because no one had recorded their contribution.

I started raising the issue, pointing out that Mary went on to be a councillor, one of the first women to do so, she was then a bailie, all the while promoting policies and practical action to advance the cause of working-class families.

Then one day, John Kane and James Adams, Labour councillors in Govan, asked me if I would chair a campaign to create something in her memory. We thought we might only get enough to erect a plaque but when we launched the campaign, the money started rolling in.

So many people and organisations responded: housing associations, trade unions, the Labour Party, former Manchester United manager Sir Alex Ferguson and thousands of small donors. People enjoyed hearing her story and wanted to see our project succeed. The statue was eventually erected at Govan Cross and is serving its purpose well – not just commemorating this Red Clydeside hero, but as a constant reminder that you can fight injustice and win.

If I look back on my political life, I would advise people never to give up if you care about an issue. Stick at it and persuade people of your case. Nothing happens without struggle, but you can win. If you don't fight, you certainly will not win. There is no benign overlord who will make things happen, it is up to you and me.

DAVE SMITH

Blacklisted

As a bricklayer in the 1980s and '90s, I was aware of the rumours swirling around the construction industry about 'certain people' being banned from employment on big sites. However, no one could prove it. That all changed in 2009, when the Information Commissioner raided the offices of the Consulting Association, a shadowy organisation funded by some of the UK's biggest construction companies. In 2011, having long since hung up my trowel and now a Labour MSP, I began to work closely with UCATT, UNITE and the Blacklist Support Group, raising questions in the Scottish Parliament, hosting debates, attending demonstrations and using every parliamentary and extra-parliamentary opportunity to expose the blacklisting conspiracy.

Dave Smith, an UCATT activist, became a great source of information and someone I could rely on for advice and support. He knew the issue inside out, as he had been a victim of the blacklist for several decades. A civil engineer by profession, Dave is a chirpy Cockney.

As a safety representative on various large projects, Dave was responsible for raising concerns with management about site welfare, safe working practices and hazards. Over time, he found himself unable to secure long-term employment, or indeed any work, even at the height of the London building boom. Like thousands of workers, he was the victim of an organised blacklist financed and run by the biggest construction companies in the country.

I COME FROM a working-class area of East London, the Borough of Barking and Dagenham. I was brought up in a council house and went to comprehensive school. My dad is an electrician and every male member of my family works in the building game, as have generations before. Like everyone else, I went into the building trade.

For a number of years there were no problems. Then, when I got involved in the union and started raising issues about safety – the lack of site toilets, asbestos, unsafe scaffolding, or whatever – I soon found myself out of work, even in the middle of a building boom.

Working in the building industry has always been itinerant and temporary. You work on a site then move on when the job finishes. You would normally get a few months out of a run, sometimes a few years, but some of the guys I was at college with were getting six months or even a few years before a move, while I was lucky to get six weeks.

A pattern emerged: pretty much any time I raised health and safety concerns or site conditions, I'd be sacked. It was as simple as that!

On a site, my role as civil engineer is important. It's effectively a lower end management job and I had an office and computer. I was the guy with the theodolite who told people where to bang a peg in the ground to set out the building and the bricklayers how high to build the bricks.

I always worked through agencies with subcontractors. At times there is a big demand for civil engineering skills, but it became obvious that even during these times when there was a lot of work, I was idle. I was defaulting on my mortgage when everyone else was working and earning decent money. While other building workers were adding extensions to their house or taking the kids to Disneyland, I couldn't even pay the bills.

I soon learned it wasn't only me – my experience was being mirrored in the experience of other trade union activists. You couldn't get a start on the big projects and any jobs you did get were on smaller projects, where the money was less. And even then, it wasn't long before they got rid of you.

When I first joined UCATT, some of the old boys used to talk to about blacklisting. They told me, 'Oh yeah, if you get blacklisted you won't get a job, they stop you from working.' Back then, I thought they were milking it and spinning me a yarn, if I am honest.

Builders tend to work in gangs, so when I couldn't get a job as an engineer I started with one of my cousins as a carpenter, but it got to the point that we would turn up on the job, fill in our details and give our NI number, and all the other chippies were allowed to start except me. It was blatant, not in any way subtle. The blacklist was real, however much those in authority denied it.

I went to politicians and raised the issue, but they dismissed it as a conspiracy theory or said I was making it up. But something was definitely going on. I and others were being denied jobs.

The nature of the work being that you don't work in the same place for long periods of time, you don't build the same bonds. My social network became my friends in the union – and they were going through the same thing. We used to meet regularly and if someone got sacked we gave them support. We were called the 'Joint Sites Committee' and we went to building sites, handing out leaflets encouraging people to join the union. During this time, I was a UCATT branch secretary, shop steward, safety rep and vice chair of the regional council.

The unions have always complained about blacklisting. Every union conference I have attended has had a resolution or debate about it, but until you have documentary evidence it is difficult to do anything. It all sounds a bit anecdotal and a bit conspiracy theorist.

In the mid-2000s, a group of three electricians from Manchester – Steve Acheson, Tony Jones and Graham Bowker – were going from one big job to another, lasting the maximum of a week before being sacked. It was obvious what was happening to them, so they had a dispute at the Manchester Royal Infirmary site and the new law courts job. They stood on a picket line for three years. Yes, *three* years! Even after they won their employment tribunal they continued picketing. They said, 'There is a blacklist and we want to expose what is going on.' At one tribunal, one of their managers contacted them to say, 'Everything you are saying about blacklisting is true!' The guy's name was Alan Wainwright. He came forward and offered these electricians a witness statement that could be used at the employment tribunal, stating that there was a blacklist and that it was run by an organisation called the Consulting Association. He stated that all the big companies were involved in spying on trade union activists and putting information on a centralised list; every time someone applied for a job on a building site, they checked to see if they were on the list and if they were, they didn't get a start.

A journalist from the *Guardian* picked up on the story. He interviewed Steve Acheson and asked why he was still picketing and the Saturday edition of the paper carried a big double page spread saying that a whistleblower, Alan Wainwright, has exposed the blacklist operating in the construction industry.

Then a shop steward from the PCS union who worked in the office of the Information Commissioner bought a paper and put it on his boss's desk and said, 'You should look at this, it looks like a breach of the Data Protection Act.' Another bit of the jigsaw and another bit of luck had gone our way. The investigating officer spent around six months getting warrants and all the paperwork together. They then raided the offices of the Consulting Association, where they found 3,213 files with names, NI numbers, addresses, phone numbers and work history – everything we suspected, everything we were looking for. That was the point it went from being dismissed as a conspiracy theory to a reality supported by solid evidence.

Lots of people played a small but significant part in exposing the blacklisting operation. It was a big jigsaw that eventually came together. No one person wins anything on their own when it comes to workers' rights. We are definitely stronger when we work together than when we work alone. The lesson is, we can't do it on our own, we are stronger when we work together, that is the essence of trade unionism. We are not looking for heroes or martyrs in the movement, we are looking to bring people together and collectively deliver fairness and justice at work.

The Scottish Affairs Select Committee at Westminster held an investigation and the chief executive of the Consulting Association was asked, 'Did the Information Commissioner take all the files?' The committee was advised they only took around 10 per cent of the files. We now know from witness statements that the Consulting Association had files covering a very wide range of sectors, including rail and offshore. They had files on environmental activists as well.

It was not only building site managers who were providing information to the Consulting Association, some of it was supplied by the police. When we first alleged that the police had provided information, some of the people said to me, 'Nah, sorry Dave, you are going too far.' But six years after we put in a complaint to the Metropolitan Police making these allegations, we got a letter back saying that we were in fact correct. The story was splashed all across the newspapers and TV. We were totally vindicated.

People had accused us of being conspiracy theorists and away with the fairies on this stuff, yet here we had the Metropolitan Police confirming everything.

Some of the reasons people were on the blacklist was incredible. My file had a copy of my safety rep card, which had been sent to the company by the union; when the company got this, they sacked me.

One of my friends, George Fuller, his file said he was 'organising a petition against homelessness and asking building workers to sign it'. One of the guys was blacklisted because 'he was wearing an Anti-Nazi League badge'. Surely we are all against Nazis? I mean, would they prefer he wore a pro-Nazi badge?

People were listed for being members of the Labour Party, attending union meetings, selling the *Socialist Worker* newspaper, or complaining about a lack of toilets, washing and eating facilities on sites. It was ludicrous.

When the files first came out, John McDonnell MP hosted a meeting with us in the House of Commons. There were about ten of us in the room, some meeting for the first time. We went around the table and we all said the same thing: 'Why aren't the unions organising a campaign? Why isn't anyone doing anything?' Then the penny started to drop that we were the people most affected and we had to become the campaign. So we set up the Blacklist Support Group, but from the start we thought, we alone won't change things. We wanted the unions involved. We wanted their support, the back-up of union lawyers, we wanted publicity, we wanted to bring in politicians. However, we were not prepared to hand the campaign over to a lawyer or politician and ask them to get on with it. Social change comes from below, not from handing things over to any politician. The people affected have to do the mobilising. And yes, it is great to have an investigation by the Select Committee and a court case in the High Court, but at the same time if even after it has been exposed people can't get jobs on a building site or continue to get sacked, as happened on Crossrail and other big sites around the country, then we have to go back to good old-fashioned industrial action. And if the trade unions, because of the anti-union legislation, can't do anything officially, well... I'm not a trade union official, I can't be sequestrated...

A bunch of us thought, come on then, we'll have a go! The result is we've occupied the head offices of Skanska, Laing O'Rourke, Sir Robert McAlpine and many of the other big construction companies who blacklisted me and my fellow workers, and we will continue to expose them as often as we can, as they are up to their necks in it. There are young electricians today who cannot get a job because they are active in their trade union. When they do Freedom of Information requests, they get back copies of emails between the companies where they talk with each other about how they are monitoring people. What are big multinationals doing monitoring union activists who often do not even work for them? It's corporate Big Brother, that's what it is.

We deployed direct action, occupying offices and picketing, bringing sites to a halt by blocking roads, turning up at shareholder AGMs with a 20-foot blow-up rat, demonstrating at black-tie events hosted by the companies, where directors and their wives were going in all dressed up in their finest... all of that made a difference, because it got publicity. If it had only been a court case or a Select Committee inquiry, we wouldn't have had anywhere near the publicity but because we mobilised 300 people to shut down Oxford Street when Crossrail blacklisted workers building three stations around Oxford Street, we got it into the public domain. It was because we got 400 construction workers outside the Grosvenor Hotel on Park Lane when the National Building Awards were going on, that we generated pushed the attention in our direction. That was key. That's when the media became really interested.

When the court case eventually came up, about 800 of us took a group litigation and forced the employers to offer a grovelling apology to us and pay compensation. UCATT and UNITE said it was the biggest compensation ever paid to their members. It was a significant thing, but compensation is not justice. A few pounds don't make up for the fact that some people were out of work for years. Having a few quid now isn't the same as having a few quid when the kids were at school and wanted to go on trips and the like.

Although they gave us an apology, we were clear that the only thing they were apologising for was getting caught. We want to see those people in court. If justice means anything, then the people who have acted illegally, who have done something wrong, should be held to account. We know who did this – it is the directors of multinational building companies who did this. In a fair world they would be in prison, but they are not. Since this happened, many have been promoted, not held to account. They haven't been disciplined or sacked – they don't think they have done anything wrong!

We are not going to give up. We are like a dog with a bone, because we take this personally. These are the people who punished my kids, put a strain on my relationship, caused me to default on my mortgage. They stopped me earning money to keep my family. Some people lost their homes, some their marriages, their health… some committed suicide. Years of unemployment is not good for your mental health.

What we want is a public inquiry. The companies will buy themselves out of a court case, but they can't buy themselves out of an inquiry. They would be forced to give evidence, that is why we want an inquiry.

The main lesson from all of this is the importance of organising. It's not just about having the right policies, having right on your side, or anything like that. It is human beings that change things, so they need to get organised. Social media is good but liking something on Facebook is not the same as organising on the ground.

For a campaign to work you need to bring people in, get them on your side and give them the opportunity to show how much they support you. Public meetings, protest, conferences and demonstrations all help. You need a core of people who will stick together and give others the opportunity to join in. If you can do that, you will get support. Do not burn people out by doing too much, allow them to aim their fire at the common enemy. We are allowed to disagree, we are a democratic movement, that is what the labour movement is about, but the movement is best when we take aim at the common enemy, whether it is the Tories, or the big bad multinationals who breach our human rights and destroy our environment or are racist. The more opportunities we give people to demonstrate our common objectives, the stronger we are. 'United we stand, divided we fall' is not a cliché, it is what we should all abide by.

I am an eternal optimist. I wouldn't be doing this if I was a pessimist. I think we can change the world. I am a trade unionist, I am not a victim.

We *can* change the world. The trade union movement at its best isn't just about pay or safety, it is about equality, justice and fairness. Who wants to live in an unequal, polluted world? I want to live in a green and pleasant environment and stand shoulder to shoulder with my brothers and sisters all over the world. I have never been more optimistic than I am now.

ALEX BENNETT

The Coal Strike – A Miner's Story

I have worked closely with Alex Bennett over the last ten years. Along with the NUM, Thompsons Solicitors and a group of retired miners, we have driven the campaign for a Scottish public inquiry into the miners' strike, seeking a pardon for those convicted during the dispute. During that time, Alex and I have become close personal friends.

Alex came from a family of miners. He worked in the Midlothian pits from the age of 15 and was chairman of the NUM branch at Monktonhall colliery during the year-long miners' strike of 1984–85. He was blacklisted and denied employment because of his union activities. Later, he served as a local councillor. He tells of the struggles and hardship experienced by mining communities during the strike.

I COME FROM a wee village called Newton near Dalkeith next to the old Woolmet colliery. I was born on 16 January 1947. The house where I was born was owned by the National Coal Board. I attended Newton Village Primary School before going to Dalkeith High School until I was 15, when I left to start work at the Woolmet pit, which was walking distance from the house and where my dad and uncles worked. I remained in the coal industry until 1997.

I remember my grandfather and da telling me about the 1926 general strike. They stole a sack of flour off the back of a lorry, not because they were thieves, but because the family were hungry. My da told me that when he got caught he was handcuffed and ankle-ironed and paraded from the High Street in the centre of Edinburgh to the court. He was fined £2, but they would have been as well fining him £200 because he never had it to pay. Someone anonymously paid the fine and he never until the day he died found out who it was that paid the £2.

My da was not all that political but he was a member of the union and could stand up for himself. My mother was more political. I had an older brother who died in 1945 at the age of 11 and my mum said that he would never have died if there had been a National Health Service. After his death, my mum became very active in the labour movement. In her day job she was a cleaner at the pit, where she worked until she retired.

I worked at Woolmet for three years, 1962–65, then went to Monktonhall, a brand new pit. There was a huge difference between the two. In Woolmet, coal was transported by hutches, whereas at Monktonhall there were wide roads and locomotives. And at Monktonhall the ventilation was far superior, which helped with health and safety. All round, the new pit felt safer. At Danderhall Miners' Welfare we have a memorial garden which records that in the lifetime of the Woolmet pit, 46 men and one girl were killed – that was between 1916 and the pit closing – whereas, at Monktonhall, ten miners have died. Ten too many, but far fewer than in the older pits. That was under the National Coal Board, not the private coal companies.

The first strike I was involved in was in 1969. I got married earlier that year and was moving into our first house at the time. It was an unofficial strike but the whole of Scotland came out, and Wales too. It was about wages. At that time, we were under a power-loading agreement and every region had different terms, there was no national agreement. It wasn't until 1972 that we had a national ballot and stuck together, voting for action to support pay parity across the country. This meant a power-loader in Scotland would be paid the same as a power-loader in Wales or Kent or anywhere else in the UK. On top of this, we got an increase in basic pay and individual rest days, and for the first time, Christmas holidays (previously we worked on Christmas day). This victory gave us confidence and made us a more solid union.

A big influence on me at that time was Michael McGahey, a leading figure in the miners' union. Joe Gormley was the NUM President and he came in for criticism from many, including me. But the best conditions we had were when he was president and worked with Michael and others to deliver better conditions. Following these victories, we definitely became more confident and more militant, no doubt about it.

In 1974, the Heath government set out to take us on and imposed a three-day week on the miners. Heath put it to the country: 'Who runs Britain? The government or the miners?' Some on the right wing of the NUM proposed a return to work, but we stayed on strike until we knew the result of the General Election. With the three-day week and power shortages, Heath's gamble failed and his government fell.

At Monktonhall, Jimmy Sneddon was the chairman of the NUM and I was the vice-chairman. In 1980, when Jimmy retired, I stood and was elected chairman. We always had a decent working relationship with the management. Willie Miller was the deputy manager at Monktonhall but when I was at Woolmet he was the chairman of the union; his father had been the secretary. He respected the union and we respected him. But they then changed the management structures at the pit, bringing in Willie Kennedy and Willie Kerr, people with no time for workers or the union.

At this time Monktonhall was one of the most militant pits in the UK. There was strong leadership and with the political balance between the Communist Party, which I was a member of, and the Labour left, we formed the Broad Left Alliance and worked well together.

Eric Clarke, who was active on the Labour left, was a regional councillor. In the contest to succeed Bill Maclean, the Scottish General Secretary who had died suddenly, the Communist Party supported Eric. We worked together and respected each other.

With the change of the management at the pit and me as chairman and David Hamilton as delegate, we would meet every Thursday. Whereas previously we had good relations, these meetings soon became a waste of time. There was a big attitude change. For example, at one point, the management were concerned that there was not enough future development or coal being driven. We brought in all of the experienced miners and we thought we had resolved the issues between us. Then at three o'clock that afternoon, after a day of discussion and problem-solving, Willie Kerr brought in the union to advise us that the new Peacock development had been cancelled. It was clear that the chairman of the Scottish Coal Board, Albert Wheeler, had intervened and cancelled the development. This was just one in a long line of bad decisions. The men had had enough and walked off the job. When the back shift came in, they refused to go down the pit.

The Coal Board refused to meet us unless we went back to work, so we called a meeting ourselves. The union agents wanted us to go back to work but the men refused. We went on strike for nine weeks and then it became an official strike.

We travelled all over the country, speaking to miners at different pits about the dispute. I went to Nottingham and spoke at the national delegate conference. I warned them that this was more than just bad management, it was coming from the top. We got a lot of support from across the coalfields and received donations of money from different pits. When we eventually went back, an overtime ban and various local disputes emerged in Ayrshire, at Seafield, Polmaise and elsewhere.

When the pit closure programme became public, we booked the Brunton Hall in Musselburgh and held a mass meeting with around 800 there. John McCormick from Polmaise spoke about the government's plans and how the Coal Board wanted to end production at his pit and many others. We put it to the vote that our delegate should support strike action at the next delegate conference; we won that vote and he was mandated.

Kinneil was the first to close, but at that time the men were not up for a fight. By the time it came to Polmaise, with its massive coal reserves, we all knew that Ian McGregor, as UK Coal Board chairman, was advocating imported coal. The writing was on the wall.

Many pits were under threat and there was heated debate about whether a national ballot for strike action should have taken place. But the argument was, why should an area unaffected by closures have the right to vote someone else in an affected area out of a job? The general feeling was that we didn't need a national ballot and the vote was carried by a big margin, by a show of hands – but maybe in hindsight, we should have had one.

When we went out, we got organised quickly, forming a strike committee, giving people different jobs. In the Lothians, I got the job of setting up a hardship fund to help those in most need. There was a lot of picketing at Bilston Glen, where one man continued to work, but at Monktonhall the strike was 100 per cent solid and we had a picket line every day.

Being responsible for the hardship fund, I saw and heard some terrible things. I had to go down to Niddrie Mill to meet one of our guys who was struggling. His neighbour had phoned me to raise her concerns. He lived on his own and all he had left in the house was a chair, a table and a phone – he had sold everything else. He had even sold his coal to the local coalman. I went to the Social Work Department in Craigmillar. They were sympathetic but were stopped from helping by what was then a Tory council. We took the man to the shops and bought him food and soap and essentials. He really was in a terrible state.

I also went to see the pit manager and asked him to give the man a few shifts on safety cover (this was sanctioned by the union) and thankfully they agreed to that.

At the time of the strike, I had two kids at school. Our family was lucky, because my wife had a job at the wire works in Musselburgh. Because she had a wage, we got nothing from the Social Security. However, as union officials, we had a decent working relationship with the DHSS and we helped many people claim benefits in the early days.

There was tremendous solidarity shown to us from around the world. We got food parcels from the Soviet Union, and many other countries donated money, toys, holidays and much more. We had members whose wives were expecting babies, so we got donations of cots and nappies. I went to one woman and told her, 'It's okay, we've got you a cot, a buggy and all the stuff you need.' She replied, 'Alex, you'd better make it two, it's twins!'

We had an arrangement with a British Home Stores branch, that when the shop closed for Christmas, all the miners' families could go in and use vouchers we gave them to them get presents for the kids.

Our picketing rota was organised by Davie Costello and Davie Hamilton (who later became MP for Midlothian). We picketed power stations and Bilston Glen pit. In the first few months there was no trouble. The local police drank in the Miners' Welfare Club and the annual police bowling competition was held at the green at Danderhall Club, so we knew them all well.

We went around the UK drumming up support, attending union conferences and political meetings, and we also travelled to Belgium and other countries, speaking to groups asking for their support. We got tremendous support from the CGT union in France, they sent us toys for children at Christmas, and unions in the US, Australia and all over the world helped. Unison gave us money to buy every household a chicken at Christmas; maybe not a turkey but every house got a chicken for Christmas dinner. We got crates of tinned food from the Soviet Union. Every striking miners' family will have had Siberian bean soup. If you've never tasted it, try it! Some people liked it, many didn't.

We set up soup kitchens to feed people. The women's support group were outstanding, they were key to the strike lasting so long. The men were encouraged and supported by their wives and partners; they were not being nagged to go back to work, even though there were huge pressures on their families. Every day in the local clubs there was a lunch put on. I will never eat corned beef again! One time, we were sent a load of lamb chops from a union in New Zealand. That was great, a break from corned fucking beef.

The strike politicised many people, from medics in the medical centre, to men in lamp rooms, who had never been political before. The strike was their political awakening, just as it was for their wives. Margot Russell, now a local councillor [who became Midlothian Council's first Older People's Champion in 2021] is a great example of that. The experience of her husband during that year drove her to become heavily involved in local and national politics. That is what it did to people.

Each of our union branches contributed money to the central strike committee and we got money from the Union HQ. From there, we decided where we would picket and what we would do.

We had argued with the Coal Board that we were due holiday pay for the Edinburgh trades holidays, as that money had been earned the year prior to the strike. The Coal Board then dangled the carrot, saying men would get their holiday pay if they returned to work. We feared some would return to get the money. Some did at Bilston Glen, not many but some, so we had to increase the picket there. We also sent a busload to Orgreave. I didn't go to Orgreave but had already been at pickets at the Hunterston Power Station in Ayrshire and at Ravenscraig. Hunterston was the biggest picket I have ever seen, also the biggest police presence. We were trying to stop scab coal on Yuill & Dodds lorries going in. There must have been 3,000 police at Hunterston. After these events, the police tactics changed. All the local police were withdrawn from the line. Police officers I played with in the pit pipe band with were taken off strike duties and replaced. Snatch squads were set up to make arrests, targeting union officials, all the time upping the ante.

I was arrested at Bilston Glen and charged with 'inciting a riot'. The law said we were allowed six pickets on the main gate. The police refused to let us join the small main gate picket and when we went back to the crowd, me and Davie Hamilton were targeted and arrested. We were taken to Dalkeith Police Station then transferred to the High Street in Edinburgh where my da had been jailed 60 years previously. I was fined £100, charged with breach of the peace and sacked.

Davie Hamilton was later arrested again for an incident in Woodburn Miners' Club. He was alleged to have assaulted a working miner. In any other circumstances he would have been dealt with by the club committee, but on this occasion he was remanded in custody for three months. When it reached court, the case lasted 20 minutes and he was found not guilty. It was a farce.

As time went on, people became destitute and there was drift back to work. One man's wife left him, he had two children. He went back to his work at Monktonhall and when he saw me on the picket line, he was sobbing and said he had had enough. I understood his plight. I could never have stopped talking to him. I felt sorry for him. His kids went on holiday to East Germany along with my two and other children and mothers, but being on his own with no pay must have been really hard. He couldn't take any more.

At Monktonhall, the NACODS (the pit deputies' union) delegate, Tammy Shields, told us that as long as there were six pickets on duty they would never cross the line. He was as good as his word. They did provide safety cover – we agreed to ensure that the pit was kept maintained and safe for when the strike was over and we could return to producing coal.

Eventually, the national executive of the NUM recommended a return to work. We met in Danderhall Miners' Club to discuss the decision and I had to chair what was a very difficult meeting. Feelings were running high and people had many different views. In the end we decided, 'We have been on strike for a year together, let's go back to work together!' We organised buses and the pipe band and the banners and the men and their families to lead us back.

Many trade unions came along to show support, as did gay and lesbian group from Edinburgh. All the kids got a day off school to attend the march.

In the Labour Rooms in Musselburgh, we set up a victimised miners centre to fight all the sackings. I was one of about 100 sacked from Monktonhall out of over 200 across Scotland.

In normal times, if someone was sacked the delegate would work through the conciliation service. If it wasn't resolved by that, the management and miners' agent would attempt to sort it out and if this still didn't fix it, then it went to the area disputes committee and then to an independent umpire – this was Jack Kane, a former Labour Provost of Edinburgh. The Coal Board refused to honour the conciliation system. We had to take forward tribunals and there was a time bar after three months. Some in other pits missed the deadline, but we made sure everyone got their paperwork in on time.

We prepared all their cases for the tribunals. John Henderson, our lawyer from Thompsons, asked us to speak to every miner going to tribunal and to make sure they were telling the absolute truth, as he didn't want the case to fall apart. Some of the stories were heard would make your hair curl. On Fridays we held collections at the pit to support sacked miners. The manager at Monktonhall, Willie Kerr, wouldn't allow us to collect in the pit, so we stopped the buses and collected that way. As a result, we were able to give every man £70 relief money. That kept us going, although it was tough.

We knew the Coal Board would have a problem with any tribunals because they had not followed the right procedures. Anyone who was arrested was summarily dismissed, no interview or hearing or anything, just a P45. They tried to do it retrospectively and called people for interview. I remember getting my letter and heading up to the pit. When the security guard, Willie Paris, saw me, he panicked and said, 'Alex, I've not to allow you into the pit, I've been told!' I showed him my letter and went through. But in the end, I was sacked. Some were reinstated and others like me went to tribunal. I won my case, but the Coal Board still refused to uphold the ruling of the tribunal. I never received any communication from them at all. I was awarded compensation, which helped, but it was nowhere near what I would have got for redundancy. I was then blacklisted for three years and could not get a job. Some of the guys were getting jobs in the building trade or at Millerhill on the railway, but I could not even get an interview.

When Albert Wheeler left and George McAlpine came in as area director, with a very different attitude about how to deal with people, things changed. I got a call from John Cunningham, head of industrial relations, who told me to get myself up to Bilston Glen as there was a job for me with AMCO, the private company who were recruiting for Longannet in Fife, and to take Jimmy Finlayson with me. So we got a start. We were back earning good money, but it was a 100-mile round trip each day and after a while I got sick of it. My wife, son and daughter were now all working, so money was not so desperate. We got paid for travelling, but that wasn't the issue. I had learned how to use the newer technology at Longannet, so I agreed to go to Monktonhall and borrowed money to invest £10,000 as part of a workers' enterprise to take over the pit. I stayed there for five years.

I was back as branch secretary of the union with Willie Kennedy, my former manager, in charge. He had good ideas, but the merchant bankers who were involved refused to take them on. The pit should have been a success. Willie and I worked well. He took me a walk one day and told me, 'Eck, as long as I'm here, you'll have a job.' It was good to be there, but it didn't last as long as it should.

I would do it all over again. Before the strike, we were among the highest paid industrial workers in the country. Mining, the pit, the club, the band, my pals – it was a way of life, a better way of life and I would do it all again! It was in my blood, bred into me from my father.

The biggest lesson from the strike is of the need for unity. Division weakens us. We were divided – Nottingham the UDM, the scabs – we did not have unity. I believe that the independence referendum has weakened the labour movement in Scotland, creating division. We need to stick together to win victories and be strong. We need unity and solidarity, or the establishment win.

I went on to be a councillor before retiring in 2012, but I continue to represent people at tribunals and help with disability and industrial injury claims and appeals. I still live where I always have and am active in the retired miners branch – it's in my blood.

DENNIS SKINNER

The Coal Strike – A Politician's Story

Dennis Skinner was born into a coal family in a coal village. He worked as an underground miner for 20 years before entering Parliament and represented his home constituency of Bolsover from 1970 to 2019.

A lifelong socialist, always on the left of the Labour Party, he refused to sit on cross party groups or go on foreign trips, and until his retirement had one of the best attendance records of any MP. Dennis played a key role during the 1984–85 miners' strike, both inside and outside Parliament, giving unwavering support to the National Union of Mineworkers, speaking at around 300 meetings and donating his annual parliamentary salary to the cause. The strike had a profound impact on him, his community his family and friends.

Here, Dennis reflects upon that momentous year and his role as an MP supporting the miners and their union during the heat of the battle.

WHEN I LEFT school, I went down the pit, a local pit near Clay Cross called Parkhouse colliery, where my dad was a miner. I think I was about 16. I do not think my father and mother expected me to go down the pit, because I had won a scholarship to a grammar school and I had been there for a few years. Then I started playing football with the pit team and cricket in the youth team. They had black fingernails, I still had that school cap on my head. I realised that I really should be with them, down the pit.

There were only 18 grammar school scholarships in the whole of Derbyshire and I was the only person in Clay Cross who got one, so naturally my parents had expected me to go to university. Scholarships were not thrown about willy-nilly, so they expected me to do what my three kids have done, but I went down the pit and I joined the lads I had been playing football and cricket with.

It wasn't long before I was attending trade union meetings. My father was very pleased as not too many people turned up at the NUM meetings in those days, unless it was voting for the holidays or something like that. I was there as someone who would be voting 'the right way' and eventually I got the same job as my father had and became the delegate for the colliery when I was around 23, which was very unusual for someone so young. I was elected in a pithead ballot and got around 440 votes against around 100.

There was a mixture of left-wing Labour and Communist Party members and supporters in that pit. There were two communist brothers called Hankinson who played a significant part in the NUM. The Derbyshire NUM meetings were held in the miners' offices in Chesterfield. There were 46 pits then, that was a considerable number.

Before I was 30 years old, I was elected onto the council. They wanted me to stand because Labour had lost control of the council to the Independents, who were really Tories. So I became a councillor as well.

That, together with being part of the NUM, resulted in me becoming the youngest ever president of the Derbyshire miners. Peter Heathfield, who became general secretary during the 1984–85 strike, was the president or vice president alongside me over that period. I then played a much more significant part in the NUM.

Around 1967 or '68, they asked me to go on the political roster to fight for the political nomination for the Labour Party in the Bolsover area. The sitting MP was undoubtedly a friend of 'Woy Jenkins', 'Shirley Poppins', 'Buck Rodgers' and 'Dr Death', the gang that formed the SDP, and he later joined them.

I had had a pretty meteoric rise in the NUM and I think my father was quite proud of the fact. I remember I was actually in the chair when my father was elected delegate of another pit called Sherland, about four miles away from

Parkhouse. He was the delegate and I was in the chair at that very same meeting. I think the family realised I had made a decent choice.

Everyone in my family was political. We had politics for breakfast lunch and tea. It would not be a dissimilar household from Jeremy Corbyn's, although his father probably said to him, 'Jeremy, would you like to contribute?' Whereas, in my house you had to fight your corner and say, 'Wait a minute, it's my turn.' But we were both from socialist families.

When I was selected to fight the Bolsover seat for Parliament, there were 13 pits and my majority was around 20,000. But the pits closed and after 1992/93, when Markham, Bolsover and Shirebrook closed, there were none left. Now, many of the miners have passed away and the situation is very different. It has become commuter territory.

I did know quite a bit about Parliament before I was elected. The NUM executive used to meet on Euston Road and if the meetings finished early, I would go into Parliament to have a look. I was very much involved in the NUM, so if there was a debate about wages or something affecting the miners I would do my best to get there. These were the days of Wilson, Heath and Callaghan, and to a lesser extent, Hugh Gaitskell. There was always a left-wing group in Parliament, the Tribune Group, later the Socialist Campaign Group. But it was never my ambition to become a Member of Parliament until 1967, when I was asked to take on Keith Kyle.

When elected, I was determined to act like a good left-winger and reject some of the politics that I had seen on display. I made three pledges to myself. One was to keep out of the bars, because that's where the press are. I'm not puritanical about it, but I know there are many loose tongues and where there are loose tongues there are right-wing journalists hanging about. If you were going down the pit to dig coal and smelling of drink, then the 'onsetter' would not let you down. If you had people walking through a lobby straight out of the Strangers Bar with the words of right-wing journalists still echoing in their ears, all sorts of things might happen. I also decided not to take part in all-party groups. I couldn't see the point of fighting Tories tooth and nail in a general election or by-election and then sitting round a table with them trying to resolve the problems of old-age pensions. I mean, the whole idea appalled me. I decided never to do that and in 48 years, I never have. The third pledge was to avoid all-party trips abroad, these so-called fact-finding visits. Interesting they never go on fact-finding visits to Greenland in the winter, though there must be facts to find! No, they always seem to go to Australia, when the test match is on. I have never been on a foreign trip either.

I always adhere to these principles. We judge people by what they do, not what they say. I soon realised that, compared to digging coal, being a Member of Parliament was a relatively easy job. As my father said to me, 'You won't have to watch the roof line in there, son!'

I thought the best way, as a socialist, to represent the people who elected me, was to be there every day and by and large that's what I've done, apart from three spells in hospital when, luckily, they caught cancer in time. Later, I had a heart bypass and a hip replacement, but in general, I have been there every day.

During my time in Parliament, we have gone through three national coal strikes. The first, in '72, I was never sure about. We had slipped behind many others in terms of pay and the government decided to set up a panel, chaired by a man called Robinson, which came to the conclusion, as they were bound to do, really, that we had fallen behind. They granted us our claim and our pay went up. Normally, you would be happy to get half, but they gave us the lot and said the claim was justified. So, we won that by a mile. We had a big celebration in the coalfields. I remember Lawrence Daly, who was the general secretary of the union – he was a marvellous speaker, one of the best I have heard – and he had been in Downing Street hammering out details of the pay claim, and someone said, 'Lawrence, get back up the stairs and ask them for free coal for the miners' widows.' And Lawrence said, 'You want me to go back up for that?' And we said, 'Yes, get it while you can.' That was the 13th claim Lawrence won, that tells you all you need to know about the power of the miners at that time.

Then in '74, Prime Minister Ted Heath decided to ask if the people wanted the miners or him to govern the country. I think he was a fool to do it. The net result was, the country voted for the miners. That was also about a pay claim.

My involvement in those strikes was to speak up in Parliament and ask questions and do a lot of meetings in and around London and talk at many of the big rallies that took place in the capital.

Thatcher was determined to close down the pits, because if she shut down the pits she would shut down the NUM and then the trade union movement. She brought in Ian MacGregor, who had swung the axe in the steel industry, and she gave him a few million quid, what was the equivalent to a football transfer fee, to bring him back from Lazard's.

As we moved towards 1984, the government claimed that only around 25 pits were going to shut, but people in the NUM like Mick McGahey believed it was nearer 75. Of course, the Tories lied to Parliament, not once a day or once a month, they were lying every day. All the ministers singing from the same hymn sheet, lying through their teeth, trotting out the same message that there was only 20 or so pits to close. It was all lies. They claimed they were uneconomic and deserved to be closed, but we knew that they were working to a plan of 75 closures. And of course, 30 years later, the Cabinet Papers proved we were right, and they had indeed lied – and that the case put forward by Arthur Scargill, Mick McGahey and Emlyn Williams was right.

Just before the start of the strike proper, I remember Mick being at a hotel in Scotland surrounded by Scottish miners calling on him to invoke the clause in the NUM rules to call upon other areas to come out and support the Scottish miners. Mick said no, because the time wasn't right. I was thinking, you're right Mick, the time isn't right. It was just after Christmas, we had to convince those miners who weren't quite sure or fully up to speed on the situation and we had to get the coal stocks down so that we could win the next battle quickly. I thought Mick called it right when we under pressure and surrounded by, I suppose, the Momentum of that time, trying to tell him what to do.

Mick was great – he called me up at the start of the summer of '84 and said, 'You're on a seven-week holiday, kid?'

I said, 'It's not a holiday Mick, I've got a lot of constituency work and a lot of meetings to do.'

'Well, I want you here, I want to fill that football stadium at Cowdenbeath.'

I asked him who was doing the meeting.

'Is it me, thee and Arthur?'

Well, he knew the phones were tapped, so he said, 'I will let you know when you get up here... but you're coming on Saturday – Cowdenbeath... Right?'

'Okay, I'll be there,' I said.

When I got there, Gordon Brown spoke, as it was in his constituency. Mick had advised him what to talk about, the stadium was full. It was a terrific turnout.

A week later, I got a call for Emlyn Williams, who wanted me to go down to Ferndale in the Rhonda to speak at a big new running track there. Again, I asked if it was 'me, thee and Arthur'.

He said the same as Mick: 'I will let thee know when you get here.'

They had obviously taken a decision between them to keep Scargill away. There were 10,000 there on the day.

On a day-to-day basis, the biggest problem I had during that time is there was not enough minutes in the day. That's the truth of it. People were coming to our house in the middle of the Derbyshire coalfield all the time, seeking help and advice. One of the most disheartening things was that I couldn't do anything about those who were in jail. MPs make law but can't interfere in the process of law. If I phoned or called at Chesterfield Police Station, the duty sergeant would ask, 'Are you his father?'

I'd say, 'Of course you know I'm not his father! I'm phoning about a young miner who has been in jail for two nights.'

'Well, get off the bloody phone – I'm telling you nowt,' they'd say.

That was the most disheartening thing. You couldn't help people in jail, the police wouldn't tell you what they were in for or anything else.

The miners themselves thought an MP could get information, get involved and get them out, but we couldn't. A lot of them were jailed for spurious reasons on trumped-up charges. In fact, most were for shouting 'scab', nothing else.

On one occasion, near Shirebrook, I was at picket line and police told me I wasn't allowed to walk on the road or pavement. I said to myself, 'They aren't stopping me in my constituency walking on the public highway.' I was close to getting arrested and this woman shouted, 'Dennis, come and walk on our wall,' and that's what I did; I walked on the wall and they never laid a finger on me.

I had to be ultra-careful with police because all through they were acting on behalf of the Thatcher government, every minute of every day. Without any doubt at all the police were totally politicised.

I was involved in a lot of fundraising during that year. I gave my wages for the whole year to the Derbyshire miners. I had to divide it into small amounts, £20, £50 or £100 to this group or another, because they were sequestrated and couldn't officially take my donation. So the women's support groups and the like received it in small amounts. Because Derbyshire was next door to the Nottingham coalfield, it was sequestrated first.

Day in, day out, I raised issues in the Commons. I thought we could win, but I knew the coal stocks were the most important thing and I used to watch them closely. When the decision was made to continue the strike through the summer, I was nervous. I thought support might cave in, but it didn't.

Then we had Orgreave and the police who were doing the overtime to buy big houses and cars off the proceeds would laugh at us; they would all be there, waiting on the coal trucks coming in twice a day, with their dogs and horses running after us. It was like getting a good hiding every day. I can't remember ever having a single good day at Orgreave. On the day of the Battle of Orgreave I didn't see what happened. You couldn't unless you were on the spot, because it happened as a breakaway from the picket line.

The picket line was like a rugby league scrum. The police would knit themselves together. There were more of them than us, they came from all over Britain. They used to goad us and laugh, shouting, 'See you tomorrow, more overtime for us.'

Thatcher was even consorting with the Libyan man Gaddafi in order to get more oil. There is no doubt they were building up oil stocks to keep the power on. It was a battle about resources. They hated Gaddafi's guts but did deals with him for oil to defeat us. I don't think she met him in a tent but she did do the deals. I also remember the NUM went out there seeking support and I asked McGahey, 'What did we get from Gaddafi, Mick?'

He said, 'Raisins, kid, just a bag of raisins.'

I'll never forget it.

I thought Christmas would be the beginning of the end.

Having been a miner for 20-odd year, I knew providing something for the kids and family at Christmas might be a turning point. But it wasn't, because by that time 40-odd countries were giving support, some in ways we never found out because of sequestration. But they had ways and means of doing it. The more I read, the more I realise just how much support we got. I found out much more about this 20 years on, when people who supported us from all over the world came together. There was lot more support than I knew at the time. Sometimes, we had to pass money to different areas in suitcases at motorway services stations, because they were doing everything to close us down.

Even after Christmas, areas like Scotland, Wales, Yorkshire and Durham were solid, although we saw some drift back to work. We had had this in Derbyshire from day one because we were next to Notts, who continued to work.

Derbyshire miners were living cheek-by-jowl next to Notts miners. Two Notts pits were actually in my constituency, Creswell and Bolsover. Gradually the UDM became more powerful. They were, of course, financed by the government and some dodgy people. My brother Gordon, now sadly dead and gone, was one of only 15 who stayed out until the end at Gedling. That's how bad it was there.

Throughout the year, I did three or four public meetings a week. I did around 300 in total and I sometimes wonder, Christ, how did I do that? There were miners' support groups in some funny places. I remember going to Bournemouth. The south coast was actually covered by the Welsh NUM. We had a huge meeting and the Welsh lads said, 'We'll take you with us to Swansea for the next meeting.' (That was my life at that time – meeting after meeting.) But the people of Bournemouth had given them so much food and so many donations there was no room for me in the minibus, so I had to get the train to Swansea.

One of the most amusing things that happened was when I gave my car to a bloke called Pete Darby, who was very active in the strike.

I said, 'Have my car for the week and drive me about on Friday when I come back to the constituency.'

So Pete said, 'Okay.'

We had this GMB meeting at Ruskin House in Surrey and on the way there I said to Pete, 'Don't go through central London, take the M25, but on the way back it will be quieter and we can go up Park Lane past Buckingham Palace, etc.'

And his lad, who was with us, jumped up from the back and said, 'Dad, Buckingham Palace! Can we stop?'

And Pete's thinking, I'm a revolutionary and throwing fucking bricks at every scab lorry in sight and here's my lad showing me up. He was red in the face.

When we got near Buckingham Palace, he said, 'Where do we go now?'

I said, 'Turn left, this road will take you to past Buckingham Palace.'

His kid jumped up again: 'Can we stop, Dad?'

Pete said, 'Sit on your arse. I've told you fucking once. No, we can't. Get back to bloody sleep.'

He said, 'Dad, Dad, you don't understand. If we stop, we can brick the place!'

Pete's face changed completely. He realised then his lad was a sound as a pound!

I used to see Arthur Scargill at meetings. He was always an aloof person, was Arthur. He wasn't just aloof during the strike, it was his nature. When we went to conference, we never knew where Arthur stayed. He was a loner. I never had any argument with him, but he was a strange character. Mick and Emlyn had more guile, strategy and tactics.

The longer the strike went on, the more meetings we did with women speakers on every platform. They had really grown and developed over the course of the year, they were fantastic. During '72 and '74, there was very little involvement of women, but it certainly changed during '84 and '85. That was one of the great things about it, the development of these brilliant women activists and speakers.

At a meeting in Wimbledon, of all places (I thought there wouldn't be many there, but it was packed), one of the women spoke to me about a fire they had had at the kitchen of the strike centre and how some people thought the UDM might have done it. I told her to say that in her speech and she did, she was crying when she said it. I told them to do the collection as soon as she finished and they raised a fortune for the cause. One of the biggest legacies of that year was working-class women's activism, without any doubt.

When the strike was lost, Tony Benn, who had been elected in the neighbouring Chesterfield constituency at the start of the strike, said to me, 'I am marching back with the miners at Markham.'

I said, 'Well good on you, Tony.'

But me, I couldn't march back. I couldn't do it... I had been so much involved in it... I had told so many people at every meeting that we were bound to win... which I had to do, to eliminate their doubts. I couldn't go to a meeting and leave them thinking that we didn't know how it would work out. I had to talk about victory and convince them in that atmosphere at that time that we would win. But we lost.

On the day the executive voted to go back, I watched the news on telly and then I went to work in the Commons. And yes, I shed a tear. The idea that we lost was hard to bear, because I knew the consequences would be even greater than anyone expected. They closed 170 pits by 1992. There's now none in the country.

When Heseltine announced the closure of 50 pits, it meant the last three in my constituency would go: Bolsover, Shirebrook and Markham. I was compelled to try and find a way to bring jobs to the area, so I came up with a plan for a new motorway junction right into the Markham pit yard. I thought, if I can get junction 29A and turn it into a business park, then at least some people will find a job. From the moment we lost, I campaigned for a Creswell business park. It's now there. I campaigned for a Glackwell business park. It's there too. And we got investments in other areas. We got Bolsover and Derbyshire councils to support the proposals. Some of the councillors were resentful, saying, 'It's not Skinner's junction, we thought about it years ago,' but irrespective of that, I came up with the idea because I wanted to develop Markham in the same way as the rest of the areas. I lobbied John Prescott when he was in government and told him I wanted 29A built and no opencast to stop it.

Shirebrook pit had to be flattened and the tip first. The East Midlands Development Council came forward with a proposal for a big factory or warehouse. They wouldn't tell me who it was and kept their traps shut until it was announced. It turned out to be Sports Direct and from the moment he came here the owner, Mike Ashley, said, 'I am not having Skinner anywhere near this place.' From the moment Ashley came, I've never seen him, I have never set foot in his warehouse. I've only seen him on the telly at Newcastle United matches. The employment practices in that place tell you everything about the man. If he had been anywhere near the strike he would have been fighting with Thatcher, no doubt about it. What she was up to was to destroy the unions, starting with the NUM, just as she did with steel, shipbuilding and the rest. All those unions are a shadow of what they were, that was the goal. Ashley is a Thatcherite to his toenails. He doesn't allow unions, apart from a small number of UNITE members, but most of the thousands of workers are employed by agencies. UNITE's membership is tiny at the plant, all office staff. Steve Turner of UNITE set it all out clearly at the parliamentary committee: all of the workers were on zero hours contracts.

When I look back at the strike, the lesson from it is that when the state can gather all its forces together against you, there is only one answer and that is to fight them. That is what happened in '84. They turned all the police forces into one, they took on the weakest areas, they set up a nasty so-called trade union called the UDM, made by the Tories, with the net result that they won, because they also used the legal system and the courts and sequestration to take control of the union's money in the regions and centrally. They choked off the money supply that helped finance the strike.

When I pass junction 29 on the motorway, I always think of Peter Heathfield picking up bags of cash to fund the strike in our area. You know, this is why they won't have an inquiry into Orgreave, because all this would come spilling out. All through, we knew we were under surveillance.

I can always remember the lesson from Mick: This is not the time! The Tories timed the strike to their advantage; they picked Cortonwood as a provocative action. I learned through that strike why it happened, how they used dirty tactics, how the state collaborated. But if anyone thinks that they can play games in an industrial dispute of that magnitude then they need to think again. They may defeat an employer if the government doesn't care too much, but if they come up against someone like Thatcher or Trump deploying the full weight of the state, then you have to be really ready.

I want the Labour Party to act as if it was 1945 again. Nye Bevan and others didn't pull ideas out of the air. They prepared for their time in government and pounced to make the changes needed. That's what we must do today.

TONY NELSON

A Docker's Tale

Tony Nelson is a scouser. As a young man he learned about trade unionism, politics and life from the older generation he worked with. As a member of a highly politicised union branch, which included Mike Carr, a future MP, and national union leader Len McCluskey, his working life was one of political and trade union activism.

In the 1990s, the Liverpool dockers went on strike to defend their jobs and conditions. Hundreds were sacked. There followed a two-year dispute when the workers received huge levels of support and solidarity from trade unions across the world but ultimately were abandoned by their then union general secretary. This a story of resilience, determination, failure and success.

I WAS BORN in Bootle, as the song goes, 'down by the docks'. I am from a family of dockers. When I started work at 15 years old, there were 15 Nelsons on the docks. It was inevitable I would work there too.

I started on the Canada Dock and I joined the 567 branch of the Transport and General Workers Union. In that branch were Len McCluskey, Mike Carden (father of Liverpool MP Dan Carden) and Mike Carr, who became MP for Bootle. It was a very political branch. We joke about it now, but instead of going to the pub when we were all 16 or 17, we would instead be sitting in the canteen talking about the Russian revolution!

As a young man I often worked nights. My job was in the wages department. I would go out onto the quayside and speak to some of the older dockers who had served in the war, some in the Spanish Civil War. Many were communists, socialists and Labour Party members – they educated me. I got more education in the first two years I was on the docks than I did at school. These people were amazing. They had been through so much in their lives and they fascinated me. This was during Heath's time in government, around 1973.

The first dispute I was involved in was when President Allende of Chile was murdered by Pinochet's fascists. A ship full of Chilean seamen came into Liverpool – they were all trade unionists. The company wanted to take the ship back to Chile. The Chileans and the dockers worked together and we refused to send it back to what had become a fascist state. The seamen were held in Risley remand centre for a while and then were allowed to stay on if they wanted. Many are still here. We still see them around Merseyside.

Our clerical branch for office staff was a campaigning branch. It was then that I realised trade unionism is not just about pay and conditions. It is about community, internationalism and solidarity.

We supported the nurses, the steel workers and many more. We once came out in support of the steel workers and when they went back we stayed out another week. I'm not sure to this day how that happened! My mates would say, 'They are back at work, why are you fuckers still out?'

I then became the convener, taking over from Mike Carden. That was on the Seaforth Dock, the main container base for all the cargo coming through. We would check it before it was moved on. They tried to separate us and break up the branch because we were involved so much.

In the '80s, when the South Africans invaded Namibia, Canada colluded with South Africa and tried to transfer uranium through Liverpool. We saw the South African containers and thought, 'That's unusual.' So we checked the paperwork (we did the customs work too) and found it was uranium tetrachloride for the Canadian nuclear industry. We called a friend of ours who was involved in the anti-apartheid campaign and he came down. He said he knew about this shipment and had been waiting on it coming through. We said we would not sign the paperwork and if anyone else signed it we were going on strike; we put the container in a separate area of the site. Everyone got involved, our bosses, the government, the HSE, etc. They told us we had to let it go. We said it is not going on a ship. The dockers wouldn't have touched it anyway. Then the Namibians came over, the ANC got involved, and we met government officials who eventually said, 'All right, we won't ship it over.' They sent a lorry for the container and we refused to load it. In the end the guy we dealt with from Namibia became the president. I tell you this to show how active we were and how much the management wanted rid of us.

All through this time, the employers and the government were working hard and planning how to get rid of the unions from the docks. In 1980 Nicholas Finney was appointed director of the National Association of Port Employers. He was determined to destroy unions in ports. The template was this. First demonise and undermine them. Say they go home early, that they are lazy. Say they are the highest paid people, they get more money than a doctor. Discredit them. And so followed a whole year of black propaganda against us in the newspapers and on TV.

The way the National Dock Labour Board operated was that the labour on the docks was nationalised and each docker registered with the government. The companies were private, but we worked for the government.

There had been a strike in the '80s, which we lost. We were all deregistered and went to work for the Mersey Docks and Harbour Company. The company then saw this as an opportunity to destroy trade unionism on the docks. The strike when it came was a long and dirty, hard fight to the death. We lost five men during the strike and so did they. Car and motorbike crashes, stress-related illness killed the others. It was tough.

The strike started when a company called Torside went into a dispute with a group of young dockers – they refused to pay them their two hours' overtime, which was in their agreement. Five were sacked and the rest came out on strike. They picketed the main gate and we refused to cross the picket line. The company said, 'You are not getting back to work,' and locked the gate. We thought we would have a meeting after a few days and they would start back, that had happened before, but not this time. They locked out around 430 of us.

In the second week of the dispute, they sent letters to 150 men asking them to come back but leaving out the trade union activists. They said, 'No way, not a chance.' We formed a committee of shop stewards and took over the boardroom of the union offices. We got the union lawyers, the assistant general secretaries and the general secretary, Bill Morris, to try and help settle it but it became apparent that this would not be over anytime soon. We started picketing all the gates. I was in charge of the pickets. The police presence was immense.

The company hired in Drake International, a famous strike-breaking firm, they provided workers during strikes all over the world. 20 of our own went in the first day that was it. Drake shipped in beds and men via sea. They started getting the port up and running again.

We built a network of support groups across the country and internationally. Bill Morris gave a speech to the men saying, 'You'll never walk alone. I will stand by you!' We were made up with that, but we later found out that other things were going on behind the scenes – all was not what it seemed.

As the port got back to work, we had to move beyond the picket line. We had to go international. So, three of us rang up New York and Sydney.

The east coast ports of the US are run by organised crime, while Sydney has a great connection with Liverpool. Lucky for us, the head of the seamen's union in the US was a guy called Whitey Dissley, who came from Bootle – he jumped ship there when he was a kid. We flew people out to meet him and the unions in Sydney. Terry and Kenny went to Sydney and three of us went to New York.

The Sydney MUA union said straight out to the ABC Line, 'We are not working on this as we support the Liverpool dockers.' The Line went bust within a few weeks.

In the US, we didn't know what to expect. They had a big limousine waiting for us at the airport. It was like what you see in mafia films. The guy we met said to us, 'You are going to the Hilton. Don't speak to anyone or engage with anyone. You will get a phone call at 7pm and five guys will meet you.' Me, Bobby Morton and Kevin Dunsburgh went to the hotel, checked in and went down to the bar. We saw these five guys come in with the pork pie hats on and long coats. They had been told they were seeing three Englishmen and I'm sure they were expecting us to have bowler hats and pinstriped suits, but instead they found us three scousers in jeans and trainers. As we started speaking, Kevin said, 'Okay lads, we'll get the ale in.' I could see them looking at each other, thinking, 'Who the fuck are these guys?' But we built a rapport based around our common knowledge of being a docker. We stayed with them until about three in the morning. We discussed what we wanted them to do and how we could take things forward. They said they were only the foot soldiers, we would meet the main man tomorrow. The next day we met Alton Ardus, the main man in the east coast union. He told us to go down to the Port Elizabeth Docks, the three of us, with some home-made placards. It was winter and bloody freezing. He said we can't be there or we will be fined, but you can.

Next day, we went down there, we handed out leaflets and almost immediately the dock stopped. We had stopped the ACL line – we couldn't do it in Liverpool, but we did in New York. That made the front pages of all the newspapers. It went on for three days. Their biggest ships left for Baltimore to try to drop their cargo. We went back to the union HQ of Alton Ardus (his union was a business union, we were a bunch of lefties) to thank him and present him with our union badge as a gesture of our gratitude – the badge read, 'Peace and Socialism – T&G region 6'. So I gave it to him and he snorted 'Peace and fucking socialism...?' and immediately lobbed it in the bin.

After that, we planned to go home but Alton flew us down to Baltimore to chase the ship and we stopped it there too. We went to North Virginia but the police told us to get out of the state in two hours or we were going to jail. Alton had little influence down there, so we left and came home.

With the ACL (Atlantic Container Line) gone, we thought we had won the dispute. The Mersey Docks and Harbour Company couldn't operate without the ACL. They said they would now go into Bristol.

In the February, I went back to America for the ITF conference with Bobby Morton – in the hotel, John Bauers said the ACL was going back into the Liverpool port. When we asked why, John told us it was a deal struck with the T&G leader, Bill Morris. He had been in touch with the shipping company to say he had to 'defend the interests of the union' and that he had other members affected. Would ACL come back if he withdrew support from the Liverpool dockers? This was within the first six months. It was now to become the battle of battles.

We went everywhere to speak to dockers. We had 97 ports from India, Australia and across Europe in dispute over our plight. The T&G officially supported us and we still received finance from them, but behind the scenes, Morris had given up on us. We got huge financial support from the US, a million pounds we got from them. The Australians also gave us a huge level of support. We were able to pay our members £60 per week to keep us going. During the strike I lost my home and my wife died of cancer. Many people died of stress. It was awful.

Every Friday without fail we had a meeting, regularly over 500 would turn up. We had guests from all over the world, people like Bob Crow, Tony Benn, Jeremy Corbyn and speakers from Japan, Sweden, the US, etc. The community helped us all the way through. We gave Robbie Fowler and Steve McManaman of Liverpool and Duncan Ferguson of Everton a Liverpool dockers t-shirt. Robbie came from Toxteth and knew a lot of the dockers. When he scored and lifted his shirt to reveal the t-shirt, we immediately sold around 150,000 of them. We got great support from Ken Loach and Jimmy McGovern who wrote the film *Dockers*. From that we made £130,000. We got 'Reclaim the Streets' involved; they were anarchists and they had all the mountaineering equipment and climbed cranes and machinery on the dock to stop it operating. They were younger and fitter than us, and very effective. It did cost me a trip to Manchester Airport where they had me in a tunnel in a protest (I was shitting myself).

Morris hated us getting these groups involved. He put a lot of money into the International Transport Federation and was working behind the scenes to end the strike. Fourteen months in, the union struck a deal with the company to ballot offering the 150 their jobs back. Twice they did this and twice the men refused to go back. It was Morris and Ray Collins, now Lord Collins, who colluded on this.

In '97, the Labour Party promised to sort out the dispute if they won the election. When they won, Blair didn't want to know. We had been in the House of Commons many times arguing our case and got support from Liverpool MPs Eddie Loyden and Bob Parry, but not from the rest. We met Prescott and soon after, the band Chumbawamba threw water over him at an awards ceremony – that was an action in support of the dockers.

We were still getting international support and money was coming in, but stopping the port was getting harder. Two and half years on, the executive council of the union voted to end their support. This was a sad day. We battled hard and six months later they attacked the Australian dockers in the same way, but they were ready because they had learned from us and they always thank us for that. I am going there in a few months to speak to their young members to educate them about our experience. That is very important. We do that regularly.

The US union had never previously helped anyone. In every port where dockers meet ,the Liverpool dispute is on the walls of the bars and clubs. In 2000 some of us went to Tenerife with our Swedish, French, Spanish, Portuguese, Australian and American colleagues – from that meeting of 15 countries we agreed to set up a new union called the International Dock Workers Council and from that small meeting the union now has 120,000 members – all dockers, average age around 32, a lot of them university educated. Because dockers' pay is high around the world, we do get a lot of clever people joining. Pay is high because of strength and solidarity – in Spain about 60,000, Australia about $80,000.

In 2010, my mate Terry and I were asked by UNITE to go back into the docks and organise the union again, so I am back in there. Some of the scabs were unhappy about this. We thought we had an impossible task, but we started by educating the young kids about trade union unionism and started to make progress, and you know what – every company on the docks is now unionised again. The tugs, the ferries, Seaforth and the rest are all unionised. We have brought them all back into the fold. We still have issues with long hours – 60–70 hours a week – but agencies like Drake and Blue Arrow have gone. This is a real success and progress for the Mersey dockers.

After the strike, we used the money from Jimmy McGovern's film to buy premises on Hope Street. The aim of the Casa Bar and community resource centre is to relieve poverty. We have raised £19 million, all put back into the communities of Liverpool. The bar does very well and pays the bills and we have theatre, and meeting rooms for every political party under the sun (not Tories of course). Every fucker meets here, the CP, ASLEF, the RMT, the Christians, the Humanists, the Judean People's Front, the United Socialist Party and their breakaway branch and everyone else. I always check the book to ensure no fascist groups or anyone like that is trying to sneak in. A few months ago we had a booking for a university lecturers' fancy dress party. We thought, good, no hassle there, until my partner, Jackie, told me it was a World War II theme. Sure enough, two turned up as Hitler. I said to her, 'Look, if there is anyone with a dodgy outfit on, lock them through the back and keep them away from the dockers who drink in here on a Friday.' A few minutes later she came back through needing a hand from me: 'Tony, you'll have to come through one of the lads has just knocked out Adolf Hitler!' Apparently, the fella said, 'Who are you calling a fascist?' Adolf decides to press charges and the coppers turn up. We went through the back to do statements and there was Eva Braun, Mussolini, Churchill and Hitler with a black eye and burst mouth. The young copper started taking a witness statement and says to one of the blokes, 'Name?' I butted in and said, 'Benito...' and this naive young copper was writing it down. The older copper cracked up at this.

There is always lots going on here, it's an independent provident society, a charity, so we can't make a profit. We use the money we make to organise welfare rights advice sessions, helping people in the community facing eviction, helping with benefits, employment rights, PIP and the like. We always put things on the walls to try to educate people and interest them while they are waiting to see someone. Just now, the theme is the Spanish Civil War. We have lots of photos and images up and people have come here to find out about their family members, their grandparents or uncles. We have a historian who helps research each individual who fought in Spain. We have digitised all the materials that have come from people's lofts and homes. This is all part of the international legacy of our dispute.

I am a better person for having been on strike for two and half years. I met some beautiful people who would have given us everything. In this country, you get so much diversity. People who are complete twats and then people who would give you everything, their last penny. They also taught me about the left – that not everyone on the left is as true as they would have you believe.

A woman from the south of England anonymously sent us her wedding ring after her husband died. She sent it to us to sell. Of course, we never sold it; it is kept in the safe so that if we ever find out who she is we can give it back.

Today I say to young people like those in Momentum, that they need to slow down. Hold on a minute. All my family work in here and support the place. A while back, we got a booking for the meeting hall for the 'Tribune' during the Labour Party Conference. I thought it was the magazine but found out it was the Tribune group of MPs. The young people who work here got wind of this and found out that Stephen Kinnock, Neil Kinnock's son was one of the speakers. The bar staff said, 'We are not serving Kinnock if he comes in!' I had an argument with them and said, 'The enemy is the Tories, not him,' but they were having none of it. We agreed a compromise where they agreed to serve them but only if they were allowed to wear their Jeremy Corbyn t-shirts while doing so.

Sometimes when I hear some young people lecturing the dockers about politics and solidarity and trade unions, I think: 'Hold on a minute, you are a kid. These people have been through a lifetime of struggles. We all support the left and the politics of socialism, but learn some discipline and your history, listen to people and educate yourself.' Many have never faced a bad boss, never worked in industry, never been through tough times. We hope people can learn from our experience, our solidarity, and come to understand why not to attack people just for the sake of it. Learn to keep your mouth closed and ears open at the right times and you will learn and develop your understanding of your politics and the world.

MARK LYON

Taking on a Corporate Giant –
INEOS, Unite and Grangemouth

*Mark Lyon served his apprenticeship with BP at the giant Grangemouth plant
in Central Scotland. He lived in a BP house, was brought up playing on the
streets around the refinery where his parents worked and went to parties in
the local BP Social Club. A welder to trade, he was proud of working with a
good employer and as a union official worked constructively with management
to help deliver positive industrial relations at the plant and good terms and
conditions for the workforce.*

*After privatisation, the giant plant was eventually taken over by chemicals
multinational INEOS, owned by one of Britain's wealthiest individuals, Jim
Ratcliffe, who was intent on cutting jobs, undermining pensions and attacking
the union. The clash saw Ratcliffe bring the plant to the brink of closure,
showing the folly of leaving such an important piece of national infrastructure
in the hands of one individual. It also allowed a hostile media to portray decent
men like Mark and his colleague Stevie Deans as the villains of the piece when
anyone with any knowledge of Ratcliffe and his aggressive anti-union attitude
knew the reality. This the story of the 'Battle of Grangemouth'.*

I GREW UP in Grangemouth, we were a BP family, like many families around the area. We could see the BP plant, which is a huge industrial site, from our house. My mum and dad had both worked at the tar plant at nearby Camelon and moved to Grangemouth when the BP plant was set up.

The new town of Grangemouth was built because of BP and my dad worked there all his days until he retired. He was a lab assistant, testing samples and chemicals and other stuff. The plant provided for us as a family. We stayed in a BP house and if something went wrong with it, for instance if a roof repair was needed, you phoned the plant and they sent the maintenance guys down on their bicycles. They would have their BP boiler suits on and they would do the repair. We were all part of something positive and there was a sense of working-class pride, which is sadly gone around the site now, I think.

We grew up in Oswald Avenue where the BP Social Club was. Everybody went there. There were many kids' clubs, Christmas parties, etc. The whole working environment and ethos at that time provided a comfortable lifestyle for families. We weren't rich by any means, but we were comfortable. It was regarded as a good place to work and one of the best paid industrial jobs around. Unskilled and semi-skilled workers were well paid too, not just tradesmen or technicians. The canteen staff, the gardeners and cleaners all had a BP contract, as did the people who emptied the bins and maintained the houses. All had in-house secure BP contracts, with a final salary pension scheme which provided for them. There was always lots of overtime. At its peak, it employed 4,500 people, now it is just 1,300.

The footprint of the plant is huge: the refinery makes petrol, diesel and aviation fuel; then you have the chemical plant making different types of plastics; and finally the 'Forties' pipeline system, the last one to be set up, which takes all the oil from North Sea and cleans it up before it goes to the refinery or is shipped to other countries and markets. It is a huge concern and by a country mile the biggest industrial plant in Scotland

I served my apprenticeship at BP as a welder and I joined the union on day one, everybody did! The convener then was a guy called Trevor George, who came along to speak to us with the full consent and support of the company and signed us all up. I have always had an interest in the union. My dad was a member and a while after I became involved he gave me a book written by Hugh Lyon. My dad's name is Hugh, my grandad was Hugh and I am Hugh Mark Lyon. Everyone in the family seems to be called Hugh, even the women. No, I'm joking about that. Hugh Lyon who wrote the book was the general secretary of the Scottish Horse and Motormen's Association. He had built that union up and in 1918 he was president of the STUC. He was my great, great uncle.

When I joined the union, there appeared to be some unwritten rule that you couldn't attend meetings if you were under 18, but I was curious about what was going on in these behind closed doors meetings which were held quite regularly in the canteen. When the meetings were going on, the apprentices had to stand outside. It was all a bit mysterious. However, I understood from shop stewards like Alex Erskine, who represented the welders and blacksmiths, the importance of collectivism. If there was a problem or an issue, you didn't go to HR or the manager, you went to see Alex and he would magically meet with the company and come back and report that things were sorted, or that some other action was needed. Our liaison with management was very, very important to the good running of the plant.

I worked in the boilermakers' workshop between 1980 and 1984 while I was serving my time. It was the most fantastic place, full of characters and a laugh a minute, but it was also shocking in terms of equalities issues. The first thing you were asked when you came through the door was which school did you go to (this indicated your religion and more than likely football allegiance to either Celtic or Rangers). It went downhill from there. No women ever worked in there. I got a job because I sat the aptitude test for school leavers. The test was only for boys. There were no women apprentices then. I passed that and got a job in the refinery. The place was an education all round – you went to the onsite training centre for a year and then to college, you learned from the craftsman you were allocated to and got a fantastic trade. My craftsman was a guy called Addie Lane, who been a whaler in South Georgia and a paratrooper before joining BP.

All of them had interesting stories and life histories, it was a real education. By 1984, the view was that less in-house labour was needed and contract workers started to come into the plant. They were reducing the number of welders and increasing the outsourced labour, so I was paid off at the end of my apprenticeship. I worked for four years as a contractor on power stations all over Scotland, doing gas work with different companies involved in offshore work.

Then in 1988, I was getting married and looking for more settled work locally. There had been an explosion at Grangemouth the previous year. One person was killed in that incident and three more in a different accident around the same time, when a fire started in a flare gas line the men were working on. As a result, they brought more in-house labour on board and were recruiting. I came back, this time as an operator. I soon became the shop steward for the hydrocracker and then union branch secretary. I was eventually elected to other union committees and to the UK-wide executive of what became UNITE. This would be from the early 1990s; I remained a lay member right up until 2014.

For ten years, I was the union convener at the plant, with responsibility for a big workforce.

Our relationship with the company was based on a healthy tension. We had a common interest in the well-being of the plant and the jobs that supported it. I have to say, we did come close to having serious disputes but never crossed the threshold. The director and HR directors worked with us and we had a good, constructive relationship. Common sense prevailed and we resolved issues between us. We were accountable to our members; they were accountable to the board and for much of the time to the government, as at that time BP was a nationalised company. When privatisation came, the government held the 'golden share', which was designed to prevent any board making crazy decisions over the future of such a strategically important national asset. One of the things Thatcher did was get rid of that 'golden share', because she wanted no interference at all in the market. This is a key point, as this left such a massive part of our country's infrastructure at the mercy of private interests.

Around 2000, BP took a strategic decision that they would get out of manufacturing, in a way that Exxon decided not to. One of the things about the sustainability of the business was that there were the three strands to it: the exploration side, where we found the oil; the refining business, that took feedstock from the North Sea; and the chemicals side. The beauty of the system was that the overall group had the whole portfolio, so if one part of the business wasn't doing as well, other parts could make up for it. The company could shift the profitability across the group for the common good. The minute you split it up, you would leave parts of the business very vulnerable. That is essentially what happened with ICI. Once it started to break up into separate parts, it became very precarious.

When BP decided to change, they initially said they would sell off the chemical plant by public offering and floated it on the stock exchange. There was great fanfare about this. But the story goes that BP had approached Jim Ratcliffe to see if he was going to buy it – and when I say buy it, this really is a misnomer, because not one brass piece came from Ratcliffe, every penny was borrowed. So, the chemicals plant went to Ratcliffe, quickly followed by the refinery. The exploration side at that time was kept by BP.

Some of these plants were built in the 1960s with old-fashioned currency, they had paid for themselves time and again, yet now they were lumbered with debt. We believed that the golden share still held by the government in such a strategic national asset would never fall solely into private hands.

Shortly after INEOS bought the plant was when I first met Ratcliffe. He had bought sites at Runcorn, mopping up ICI facilities and some BP sites, cutting terms and conditions, that type of thing. When we visited one of the former ICI sites organised by the GMB union, they said to us, 'Welcome to hell!'

It was a joke at first when they told us the parable of the Apple and the dinner money. If you give the school bully your apple, he wants your dinner money; and if you give your dinner money, he wants your bus fare home; and if you give him your bus fare home, he wants your grannie's stair lift. It was only at the point where you stand up and say, 'We are not having this,' that he backs off.

We were alarmed. None of us wanted to move away from BP. It was a paternalist company we had known for decades. In the main, they looked after people. However, we felt a bit betrayed. The community had put up with the noise, emissions and unsightly nature of the place, and all of a sudden, a strategic decision had been made – and they were off, gone.

We didn't know that much about Ratcliffe when he came to the site, but one of his first declarations was that he wanted to dismantle our pensions. We said, 'Look, this pension scheme is 100 per cent funded, the company is profitable, why on earth would you want to do that?' It appeared that this was a formulaic approach, one of the first things he does when taking over .It didn't matter whether the company was making lots of money or not, the pension had to go. Instead of being an excellent place to work, Ratcliffe wanted it to become run-of-the-mill. That was his message. We asked about investment and he said he had plans to build a biodiesel plant. Well, if he did plan to build it, I don't know what's happened as it is nowhere to be seen. All they have done is close different parts of the plant down since they arrived. At the first meeting, Ratcliffe came across as very arrogant and unpleasant. He sat side on to us and did not engage. We spoke up and said we had a good relationship with previous management and wanted it to remain that way. We said we won a seat at the table to be involved and to continue working positively with the company. This was dismissed out of hand with the words, 'It's not the type of company we are.'

One of the first things that happened when we transferred over was to end the share options for employees. Now squire, as good socialists we should never have indulged in the preferential scheme which gave workers two shares for the price of one but we left our principles at the door as it was worth a lot of money and helped us buy a new car or go on holiday. As a private company INEOS didn't have preferential share options for staff. So, when the TUPE transfer took place there was no way of transporting it across. We said, 'We are not willing to accept this loss. You have decided to buy this company with all its liabilities and we see this as part of our terms and conditions.' Every year when we had wage negotiations, the employer always raised the pension scheme and they took the shares scheme into consideration. To cut a long story short, Ratcliffe refused to move on this. We had a ballot that came out almost 100 per cent in favour of taking industrial action. The company then backed off and gave members a £3,000 payment, £3,000 onto the pensionable salary and £3,000 the following year as compensation for the shares scheme going. That was the first disagreement we had with them.

They kept raising pensions and we kept saying the scheme was fully funded and there was no need to change the pension as they were making money.

We then came to 2007, 2008 and that was when the pensions strike took place. Ratcliffe was said to have given in too easily on the shares. It seems he never got over it and was determined to exact his revenge on our pensions.

So, on the 26th and 27th of April 2008 we ended up on strike. It was a high-profile event and it was all over the media. One of my mates who was in New York at the time turned on the telly and saw my face all over it. It was a huge event. The company backed down and we came to an agreement where we kept our final salary pension, but not for new people coming in. The really honourable position that members took was that that was not acceptable, they wanted the same pension for everyone. To this day people say to me that the dispute was not about *our* pension. And it wasn't, it was about the pensions of those who would follow us into the plant. That was indeed a very honourable position to take.

Before we went on strike, and this is important, because of the hazards that are there, we agreed with the company that we would take the plant to a position where it was not producing. But from the floor of a mass meeting came a principled point, which was agreed, to provide labour to ensure the plant was safe and ready to start up again when the dispute was over. We were the competent people to do that. As far as we were concerned it was our plant and INEOS was a sort of unwelcome visitor in our town and in our work. We hope they won't always be here, but *we* will, so we have the greatest interest in looking after this place. At the mass meeting, one of our members said, 'Why don't we put a full shift out, instead of imposing the responsibility on just a few people?' So, when we were on strike we had a full shift out ensuring there were no fires or danger of deterioration in the plant. That was a really honourable and responsible thing to do. When we went to ACAS to try to negotiate an agreement, it was clear that INEOS were determined to have this strike and the only thing we agreed upon was the model of maintenance cover that we proposed.

We won that dispute easily and we could also have said there would be no changes at all to the pension scheme, but being pragmatic we did accept some changes. Part of our thinking was to allow the company to walk away with a bit of dignity. There was no currency for us in humiliating them, so we just moved on after that with no triumphalism or anything like that.

In the run-up to the 2013 dispute, life had gone on but it was obvious that the company wanted revenge on the union. They were vindictive towards us. They scrutinised every penny invested at the site and kept making threats about the future. They reduced the number of staff and introduced arduous processes for any in-house recruitment of labour in an effort to keep people off the pension scheme. The atmosphere wasn't good. Then they came and said, 'We are going to impose changes to your pension.' We had eight or nine mass meetings with our members and they were up for some sensible changes but not what Ratcliffe was proposing.

Around the same time, the Falkirk Labour Party selection process came up to choose the successor to Eric Joyce, the disgraced local MP. Karie Murphy, a long-standing trade unionist, came to us and presented herself as someone who wanted to take forward an industrial agenda very much in line with our thinking. She wanted to put her name forward to replace Joyce. At the time, Joyce was clearly ill, but equally his politics were not ours. Karie presented a completely different picture of what a local MP would be like and to us she said and did the right things. She went to various industrial sites, like ours and Alexanders, the bus makers in Falkirk, and she spoke to the workers. We had Michael Connarty as MP in the East Falkirk constituency, who had supported us solidly in all his time in Parliament. He did a fantastic job for us.

As the contest to succeed Joyce kicked off, we came out in support of Karie and some of the comments and statements around the selection became ridiculous, with the Labour leader, Ed Miliband, and others playing a less than admirable role. As the Labour Party selection contest got under way, David Cameron tried to exploit the controversy surrounding it in the House of Commons, claiming my colleague Stevie Deans was a rogue trade unionist who was trying to fix the selection contest. Now around that time, we put forward delegates to the constituency parties – not as a fix, they went on because they wanted change. The irony is that Stevie Deans got an award from the Labour Party for recruiting so many new members and then was suspended for doing so. Stevie took on the chair of the local party and I supported him. He knew he was taking on a role where there were a lot of vested interests going back decades. I asked him if this is what he really wanted to do? But he took it on. He had a lot of wrangles. Some of those people made completely false allegations about ballot rigging and the stacking of the local party, and the hostile press lapped it up, helped by some senior Labour people.

INEOS saw this as their big opportunity. They used it to attack UNITE at a time when they were seeking confrontation over the pensions issue. They suspended Stevie from work. The disagreement we had with them was about pensions, but the dispute became about their treatment of Stevie. It was victimisation of him as a trade union official. The members knew what was going on and what INEOS were up to. As full-time officers in the union, we used our influence in a principled way. For example, where there were environmental constraints that put us at a competitive disadvantage to, say, Germany, we lobbied MPs on that, just as many companies, workers and unions did. We were looking after the interests of our members and in doing so the company benefited. There was an understanding and an unwritten agreement that we could use the company email system to send emails to MPs with an interest in these issues. These were political emails and the company didn't mind because they gained from our actions. However, INEOS suspended Stevie for using the same system to send other political emails. It had been no secret he was doing this.

When the company moved to dismiss him, this changed the dynamics of the dispute. It forced our hand to move more quickly than we wanted to. We started with an overtime ban, which had an impact. But Stevie resigned his position because of the way he was being treated. His health was poor and he was not in a good place at that time. He knew he would be sacked, so he resigned.

It came to a point where, in line with our members' wishes, we gave them notice we were going to go on strike and issued them with strike dates. It was clear this was part of their plan. People have asked, did we fall into their trap? I still maintain there was no real choice. Even though we knew the risks and all the angles they were coming from, we had no choice, because the alternative was to abandon Stevie, who had been treated so badly. To cave in would have weakened us in the pensions dispute too. We didn't want to move to industrial action, but we did.

INEOS immediately rejected the approach we took previously to keep the plant running and maintain it ready to resume production. They crashed the plant down to a cold state in a way we considered unsafe. We met with the Health and Safety Executive and they counselled that the plant should be managed in the way we proposed, but the company rejected this. Bizarrely, they also wrote their assets down to nothing. These were plants worth millions, described as worthless. On the refinery side, PetroChina had taken up a 51 per cent stake. At the time Ratcliffe was doing all this, they must have advised INEOS that they wanted no part of his action. INEOS then put out a so-called 'survival plan'. It was as if someone who hated their own workforce had sat down and written up the worst list of conditions possible. People who were ill would lose their sickness benefits – this was a few people a year, often terminally ill, who would now be losing the financial security we had negotiated over the years. How would this be crucial to the 'survival' of a multi-billion-pound business? They also, in my opinion, amplified a situation with feedstocks.

The North Sea is currently producing less gaseous stock – that is, less gas and more liquid is being produced. The chemical plant needs gas, however it was still running at full pelt with the gas coming from the North Sea and we had tie-ins with the Mossmorran plant in Fife and so there were options to ensure continued productivity. INEOS put out the survival plan to our members and by 60-odd per cent they rejected it. The plan would have taken away the pensions scheme, replacing it with a massively inferior defined contribution scheme; £2,500 reduction in shift allowance for all shift workers; and overtime rates dramatically reduced. If you sat down with a piece of paper and asked yourself how we can exact revenge for 2008, then this would be the list you would have drawn up. The members, quite rightly, rejected it overwhelmingly.

After that, a guy called Colin Mclean was brought in to be the hatchet man. He came to a mass meeting and told the workforce that they were closing all the plants down. The chemical plant would be in administration by Monday and that was the end of Grangemouth. Of course, this was designed to terrify people. It was the action of a bully. We had anticipated this move, but now we had to make a huge decision, one of the most difficult I have ever had to take, and that was to save the plant.

My own assessment is that the plant would never have closed and that this was a threat. I say this because when INEOS bought one of the ICI plants in Runcorn, they had asked the Labour Government to give them £50 million and claimed if they didn't get it, the chlorine plants would close down and there would be a danger to drinking water across England. I think the police should have been called in on them at that time for trying to hold the country to ransom. If someone is threatening the water supply for £50 million, this has to be a criminal issue. They had form on issuing threats, but back at Grangemouth we had to advise our members that, despite this being an awful proposal, we were going to have to move on it to save the jobs. As predicted, after we said we would accept it, they announced that the plant would stay open.

The mass meeting was awful. It was emotional and people were very angry at what Ratcliffe had done, but we all understood that there was little we could do about it. It was accepted. Now, at various points I have questioned myself and thought, well, maybe we should have stuck it out, closed down the refinery and occupied the site. Some on the far left have made this point, but I don't accept that. We could not take a gamble with all of these jobs. If you are faced with a man with a gun in a stick-up, the sensible thing is to hand over your wallet and go after him later on. There really was no choice as far as I am concerned. It was a dreadful situation. They gave us 45 days so-called consultation on their changes. I had sent a note out in support of Stevie Deans highlighting the dreadful treatment of him and asking the workers to send him messages of support and solidarity. The company used this against me and held an investigation into me. They had started to refer to Ratcliffe as 'the Shareholder'. It was a bit like a James Bond film, they told us we were not allowed to use his name and only refer to him in these terms. We referred to him in other terms not altogether polite, I can assure you. They took disciplinary action against me for sending this note out, something I had done on numerous issues over the years without any problem ever being raised. They gave me a final written warning and wrote into the 'survival plan' that there would no longer be a full-time trade union officer on site. (We had never asked for a full-time officer – BP had asked us to go full-time because it was helpful to them.) And also, no one could be a shop steward if they had received a final written warning. I kid you not!

They then they brought in this six-foot six Irishman called Declan Sealy to deal with us and he used the type of language that if it was used in the pub, there would have been a very different outcome. He spoke to people in a very aggressive way calling us a 'disgrace', saying, 'You need to listen to me', 'You have brought this site to the brink of collapse'.

He carried out my disciplinary hearing around Christmas time. I was told to move away from the office where I was working, to a rail terminal. This was designed to isolate and humiliate me, but I was determined to return and to rebuild the union branch for the future. I came back for one shift and got an email saying they were sending a courier to my house with a letter. I knew right away what was coming.

What had happened was that after they announced the site was to be saved, they followed up with another announcement of a number of other job losses. They hollowed out the site.

Hundreds of jobs were lost, both for contractors and in-house. Pat Rafferty, the UNITE regional secretary, asked me about the closures and gave the information to the *Daily Record*. By now this was old news and we all knew about it, but this was used as one of the reasons to sack me. Our legal team was openly laughing at the ludicrous case INEOS had put together. Of course, it was no laughing matter for me, as I was out of work with a house and family to keep. I had worked without a break in employment from the age of 17 and now I was out of work, sacked by Ratcliffe. We told them they would do huge damage to the business and that is what happened, as hundreds of skilled workers left. They could barely keep the plant going. Many of these workers went abroad, to the Middle East, Azerbaijan, etc. They were highly sought-after. Employers set up in a local hotel to recruit BP workers.

Within a week, we had lodged papers at the employment tribunal service for 'interim relief', which means that, if successful, you are reinstated to employment with pay and pension reinstated pending the full hearing.

This was successful and it was a joyous day. INEOS sent Ian Fyfe, an HR manager, and I was represented by our barrister, who I call 'The Mighty Engelman'. He dismantled the INEOS representatives piece by piece. It was actually very funny. The INEOS solicitor said that I should have controlled Pat Rafferty, then changed his mind to: Pat Rafferty should have been controlling me. They produced so much rubbish, at one point saying I wouldn't toe the line! The tribunal chairman nearly fell of his chair: 'Shouting toe the line, toe the line! This man is a trade union representative, his job is not to toe the line!' At which point our solicitor passed round a notepad on which he'd written 'This is painful.'

At the end of the tribunal, members asked Philip Engelman if he had any comment on the INEOS case. He said, 'Only to say that the entire case is chaotic and contradictory.' And of course, right away I was reinstated and stayed there until the full tribunal came up. We wanted an industrial settlement, so wanted it to go to the full tribunal. INEOS offered money to settle but I wanted an industrial settlement too. We only settled when the trade union agreement was reinstated.

INEOS had to send out a communication advising that UNITE were the recognised union and that they would support trade union membership, and UNITE got access again to inductions to recruit new staff. That was the most important part for me. And while I was away from the site, the members insisted I continue to chair the branch and I stayed in that role up until just a few months ago. I now work as a full-time trade union organiser with UNITE.

I learned a lot from that time. No one has asked themselves more than me, what could we have done differently?

We could have done some things slightly differently, but I doubt we could have changed the outcome.

What I have learned is that we need political change. We need to shake off the political constraints upon us. If someone with no money can come in and borrow cash and buy up a vital piece of industrial infrastructure, dismantle half of it, hold workers to ransom over their jobs and take their pensions off them, then there is something seriously wrong with the system. At the time there was no political intervention. This has to change.

I hope we can get the political change that we need, decent legislation with protection for working people we are vulnerable. I'd like to see the Labour Party argue to devolve employment legislation. I think we could force change with this. And if we get into power we have to see real change, and then optimism would increase a great deal.

'ANDREA'

The Spycop and Me

Andrea (not her real name) was born and brought up in Ayrshire. Her father was a well-known trade union activist. A trained nurse by profession, she moved to London in her 20s to work in mental health and drug and alcohol outreach. A member of the Transport and General Workers Union, she became involved in workplace trade unionism and befriended a number of people on the radical London left scene and fell in love with one of them, a man called Carlo Neri. Andrea and Carlo moved in together. They socialised with and campaigned alongside many well-known trade unionists, left-wing lawyers and political activists.

Unbeknown to Andrea and her circle, all was not as it seemed. However, it was not until almost ten years after she and Carlo met that the Spycops scandal broke and the extent of Carlo's deceit was revealed. Andrea's remarkable story shows how far the state will go to clamp down on those whose only 'crime' is to fight for a more equal and progressive society.

I WAS BORN in 1972 and grew up in Prestwick as part of a working-class family. I lived with my granny until I was five. She had the first council house built in Prestwick, which was very exciting as these were new, modern, well-built houses with inside toilets, kitchens and bedrooms.

My dad worked on the railway and later at British Aerospace, where he became a prominent trade unionist as convener of the plant in the town. He was in the Amalgamated Engineering Union.

I grew up in a political, left-wing family. I think Dad was in the Labour Party at that time, he would have been close to people who were in Militant. I'm not sure if he himself was a member but some of his friends certainly were.

We didn't have a phone growing up as he was convinced it would be tapped. I think he had a few run-ins with the police because of his activism, so he didn't really trust them. As a teenager this drove me daft, but I just had to live with it.

Being part of the union was a big part of our family and community identity. Prestwick was an ex-mining town with a strong sense of its history and place in society. I had an ambition to go to art school but at the last minute changed my mind and went to train as a mental health nurse. I worked at a local mental health hospital for a while, then in the Royal Edinburgh hospital. In my early 20s, I left to work in London where I went into outreach work with rough sleepers with complex needs, mainly related to drugs and alcohol problems.

I loved my job and worked with an organisation called Thames Reach for six years. I specialised in working with rough sleepers with addiction problems and became a deputy manager, helping develop new specialist services. At the same time, I undertook further study in counselling and drug and alcohol studies. I was happy there and was active in the Transport and General Workers union in my workplace.

Whilst there I made good friends with a man called Dan Gilman, who was the T&G workplace rep and well known in the London trade union scene. We became friends and socialised a bit outside of work. It was through Dan that I met Carlo Neri.

I split up from my long-term partner of 12 years when I was 30, so I threw myself into work and into a bit more activism to fill the gap in my life. Through Dan and a person I worked with who was active in the Socialist Party, I met a new circle of friends who were all active on the London left. I was not a member of any party but many of my friends were. My biggest focus was my work, but my personal friendships became political and of course, I had grown up with this type of politics, so I was comfortable with that. It was natural for me.

Work was going well, the new services I set up were a success, and I had many friends but I was still single following my relationship breakdown. One Saturday in September 2002, I had arranged to meet Dan at a mass demo against the First Gulf War. Dan was with a bunch of activists and he introduced me to Carlo. He had been on the scene for around a year, becoming good friends with people like Dan and Steve Headley from the RMT, and Frank Smith from the Blacklist Support Group, among others.

About a year before this, Carlo had come to my house with Dan to drop off some packing boxes, so when I met him on the demo I said to him, 'Oh, have I met you before?' and he said, 'No I don't think so, I don't think you have.'

I said, 'Remember you were with Dan, you dropped off some boxes.'

He said he 'couldn't remember', which I thought was a bit odd.

He then said his mum had died around that time and maybe he wasn't thinking clearly.

However, from that day on we hit it off and became inseparable.

He was of Italian stock but born in Islington, having moved back to Italy when he was 15 following his mother's illness. His parents were working-class and left-wing, they ran a café in Bologna. Carlo returned to London when he was 31. This was the story he told everyone.

He knew London well. He travelled around the city as a locksmith and was especially familiar with North London. He had a strong London accent but also spoke fluent Italian and was interested in left-wing politics. His backstory did not raise any questions or suspicion.

After his mum died, he said his relationship with father had deteriorated. His sister lived in Peterborough but had a number of issues of her own to deal with, so I never met either of them. By December 2002, he had moved in with me.

He worked days with a locksmith company called 'Frankey', which still exists. When he moved in, he changed all our locks and many of my friends' locks. He was very handy. He did lots of jobs for friends and was very practical and helpful. People liked him.

On Hogmanay 2002, three months after we met, he asked me to marry him, getting down on bended knee at a party we were at. We had champagne and a lovely night celebrating with friends. Carlo was very generous and a good cook, so we had a great celebration with lovely food and wine. It was wonderful. He rang my mum to tell her personally. We had been to Scotland a few times to meet my family and they all liked him.

We had been supposed to go to Italy in the September, but my gran was very ill, so instead I went to Scotland for three weeks. He joined me just after my gran's funeral and for my sister's graduation. My family warmly welcomed him because he went out of his way to befriend them. He quickly built a great relationship with them, they loved him and he them. He was kind, generous, caring and interested in them; he never met my dad, as we were estranged by that time. Carlo was accepted into my family and friendship circle very quickly. He never forced his views or politics on anyone and was gentle and diplomatic. He was an easy person to be around. Introduced to workmates, family or friends he easily integrated into each group.

Everything was going well in our relationship, but he became bored with his job and spoke about becoming a paramedic. He loved motorbikes, so a motorbike paramedic was his dream job. However, he took up a new job with an Italian food company that imported really nice wines and foodstuffs. He said he got the job through family contacts and started travelling a bit more, and would be away maybe two nights a week. He always came back with all of this wonderful food and wine and expensive treats, not normal run-of-the-mill stuff. Then, just before he moved in, he told me had a child, a little boy called Ben (not his real name). He said he was estranged from his son's mum, who had just been back in touch to say she wanted Carlo to be part of Ben's life. He had not seen Ben for about a year and half – he was really tearful and upset when he told me all this. He said he felt ashamed. He put up pictures of Ben and his sister and his mum (these were real people in his real life, but later I established this was not their identity). He then started to travel to Cornwall to visit Ben and I was very supportive of this. Every other weekend he went to see the boy and a few times a week he was away – maybe four to five days a fortnight he would be away with work or visits to Ben and this was all perfectly acceptable to me.

In summer 2003, we had a two-week holiday to France planned. He was going to drive and we were very excited as we were going to see the Tour de France. Carlo was into cycling, it was all going to be great. The day before we were due to go, we were all packed, when came home and said, 'I can't go. I'm really sorry, my dad has had a stroke. He is very ill, I need to go to Italy.' Which he did, ringing me every day when he was there. He returned home after around two weeks, sad and down. Things were a bit different when he came back but not bad.

At Christmas, he went back to Italy. We had arranged a party for New Year when he returned. He then called to say his dad was dying and he couldn't return. Then at around 2 the next morning he called to say his dad had passed away and that he would be staying for the funeral, and because I did not know anyone there was no need for me to go. He stayed for another ten days before returning.

When he came back, he looked very different. He had lost a lot of weight, he had grown a big beard, his hair was longer, his eyes were different, and he was acting strangely. Obviously, he had lost his father and this had affected him. Then he then told me that on the evening after the funeral, his sister had confided in him that his father had sexually abused her. This was a huge revelation and a complete shock to him. He said he was devastated and felt guilty and shattered.

Carlo became emotionally distant and quite volatile. He would disappear for days on end. Once he left for a week and was out of contact. His phone was off and when he returned he said he had been arrested and kept in jail in

Italy for 'pissing on a police car'! That is what he told me. He seemed unwell and later he texted me to say he was suicidal. This was beyond stressful for me. I had no idea what he might be up to next. In June 2004, he moved out of the flat saying, 'This is not fair on you.' He took all his stuff and moved in with Steve Headley. His move was in hindsight like a forensic operation, everything down to the last spoon was removed from my house. Every bit of his life disappeared from my life.

He came back two weeks later and said, 'I still love you.' We texted back and forward for about another six months. We saw each other maybe two or three times a week in that time. The breakup was not about either of us seeing someone else; it was because he was having psychological problems, because of the guilt of not knowing what had happened to his sister. I believed all of this and so did our friends.

Prior to this, we had been going to move to Hackney and into a two-bedroom flat, so that he could bring his little boy to stay with us and we could be near our friends, but because things were unravelling that didn't happen. So, I moved in with a friend in South London near work, as I had nowhere else to go. I was moving away from my political friends and was socialising more with people from work. Carlo told people that I had kicked him out, which wasn't true. I only found this out about a month ago, via a conversation with Steve. He was also planting little bits of information with people that were fracturing some friendships within our circle. He did it in a subtle way and people began to lose trust in each other. But all of us believed his story about his child, his dad dying, his health.

In November 2004, he sent me an email saying it was all over and he wouldn't be seeing me again. And I never did. Around a year later, I met a mutual friend at a party, who told me that apparently Carlo had moved back to Italy and had a bad motorbike accident; he had survived but was badly injured. No one could contact him. His phone number and email address didn't produce any response.

I moved on with my life. I continued working and settled down, had children and went to live in Folkestone on the south coast. I lost contact with Dan and Steve and the others, although I was vaguely aware of what they were doing. I never saw them socially or via work.

Then, unexpectedly, in 2015, I got a message asking if I would speak to some of my friends from that time about Carlo. A guy called Dave Smith, who I didn't know, wanted to meet me. A few months before that, another friend had given me *Undercover* to read. The book came from a someone who was in the Socialist Party. She said, 'You must read this. It is bloody amazing – this stuff about undercover officer Pete Frances – or Pete Black – will blow your mind!'

After I read it, I told her, 'I think this happened to me too.'

She said, 'Don't be crazy, are you mental?'

I said, 'I'm telling you, I genuinely think this happened to me!'

When I read the story of the experience of women who had been befriended and lured into relationships with 'Mark Jenner' or 'Mark Cassidy', it sounded so similar to my situation with Carlo. Falling in love, settling down together, the relationship developing, followed by his mental breakdown and then leaving. These women experienced exactly the same pattern of events.

I had no evidence I was a victim other than reading this book and thinking, bloody hell, this is weird. I didn't do anything about it, but it kept running through my mind. Then the others contacted me, Dave Smith who was doing a lot of the research and then Steve Headley and Dan and Donal from the Undercover research group. I arranged to meet them in London the following week. They said they suspected Carlo was an undercover cop and that they were trying to put all the pieces together and would I help them? Had I not read the *Undercover* book, I would have thought they were mad.

The research done for the book had started the ball rolling and many in our circle had started to wonder about the way Carlo had just disappeared. There was the suspicion that something wasn't right, but no one could say what. The 'Mark Jenner' story was out by that time, as were the other women's stories. 'Jenner' had befriended trade unionists and appeared on picket lines and had had relationships with women involved. It was all so familiar. We all had our own experiences and little suspicions, so we sat down and started putting things together. Donal and Dave were convinced Carlo was a cop, but they didn't know yet who he really was, or what had happened to him. I gave them all the information about our time together, what we did and where we went. Donal started to piece together the evidence and clues Carlo had left behind.

When he was with me, Carlo had been on the electoral register, so they looked for other 'Carlos' who were connected to people we knew. They suspected he had ended up living with a woman he had had a brief relationship with before me. The researchers ended up finding them on the electoral register for East London. He was using the name, 'Carlo Sorrachi'. The undercover cops always used their real first name so that they could answer to it naturally, without being surprised or confused. The surname is always fake. Some officers used the identity of dead babies. Carlo didn't, but others did. He joked that his name was really 'Charlie Black', the English translation of 'Carlo Neri'. 'Peter Frances', another officer, was 'Pete Black' – so there was maybe an in-joke or instruction from the top about 'Black'.

We found out that Carlo's real family lived in London, not Italy, and ran a lovely deli and restaurant business in Hampstead. They had a genuine food import/ export business. We have no idea if they knew anything about what Carlo was up to. During the current public inquiry, the family made a submission, raising concerns about the potential impact on their business.

It turns out Carlo's real wife and son lived about 15 miles away from us in London, not in Cornwall. In 2016, I did an interview with BBC *Newsnight*. The journalist went to the house where Carlo's now ex-wife lived with her new husband, and broke the news to her. Understandably, her main concern was about the potential impact on the children. Her reaction was so calm and together, it made me think she might have been briefed beforehand, but I was later advised that she didn't know what Carlo had been doing until the *Newsnight* reporter told her. All she knew was that he was doing dangerous police work and was saving the country or the world! She had no real clue about the extent of his double life.

My emotions were all over the place. I felt stupid and ashamed that I had fallen for Carlo's deceit. I couldn't believe that, although I worked in mental health, I had fallen for his fake breakdown. How could that have happened? I then found out that his wife was pregnant with their second child while he was with me. This, despite the fact he told me he wanted a child with me – that blew my mind. He had this entire family unit just 15 miles away from the home we shared. He must have been going there when he claimed to be working as a locksmith or in the food business. His wife must have thought he was at work at night. I questioned everything. How could someone who appeared to love me so much do this? I started to question every part of my life and every single thing he said or did.

Thinking back to the time Carlo left, I came close to a breakdown myself. At one point my step-dad drove down from Scotland and bundled me into his car, wrapped in a blanket. It took me a long time to recover and I was very lucky to keep my job, but all this was going on when I should have been developing my career and seeking promotions.

I am absolutely clear that I have been the victim of state-sanctioned rape and so have all the other women who gave consent to someone who did not exist. The crown prosecution service has said they won't prosecute, but they should. Carlo was not a random married man who acted in this way, everything he did was in the full knowledge of his unit and his senior officers. Senior officers went wherever their field officers went, we now know this from the public inquiry where anonymised information confirmed this. The police chain of command approved it all. Whether I was in Ayrshire or Glasgow or London, Carlo's cover officer was there too. It was all part of the 'tradecraft' manual that outlined what they could do in the field, including having relationships with women.

I am confident in using the term 'state-sanctioned rape'. I used to struggle with it, as I have worked with rape survivors and survivors of sexual violence. But clearly I did not give consent to a Special Branch Officer who I knew nothing of. I did not give consent, I was duped. This is a hugely important point.

In 2011, the original eight women set up the campaign group Police Spies Out of Lives. It doesn't exactly trip off the tongue, I know. They took the legal case following the exposure of 'Mark Kennedy' – Helen Steele, Alison and Rosa and the others came together and realised that they had similar stories involving undercover cops, including Jenner, Lambert and Boylan. They engaged Harriet Wistrich as their lawyer and took a case against the police, who issued a 'cannot confirm or deny' statement.

Things changed when 'Pete Frances' turned whistleblower. He said, 'I was Pete Black and I infiltrated political and social justice organisations.' These women fought their case for four and half years until they were given an apology and a financial pay-out, but only the eight have had their cases addressed – all the rest of us are having to jump through hoops and wait for justice. I launched my case in January 2016 and am having to go through hell to take it forward. They have made it as difficult as they possibly can. I recently had to meet a forensic psychologist appointed by the police to go through my entire life yet again. I didn't want to do it but I had to. I asked for a female officer, because I was going to be talking about trauma and sexual assault, but they insisted I saw the individual of their choosing – a male. It was awful. They are trying to stop me at every turn, using all available tactics, including institutional misogyny, and they will keep doing it.

The campaign has really developed and we are getting support and affiliation from trade union branches and councils. We have raised the profile of the campaign and built the profile of the issue. I have thrown myself into it and become an activist again in my middle age. I didn't expect this to happen. I'm now more active than ever and I am totally committed to the campaign. It has brought together trade unionists, environmental campaigners and local grassroots activists. We women were targeted because we could provide access to industrial, anti-racist, anti-fascist and environmental campaigns. Now we have linked up with the Blacklist Support Group, who represent workers Carlo and Jenner infiltrated, ruining the lives of so many innocent people. Almost all of the people I was with in the early days were blacklisted. I don't know why, but I was not on the list, I have checked.

The public inquiry into the actions of undercover police in England and Wales is ongoing. The police involved are being given anonymity. This means that people who have been affected but have not yet realised it will never know, as names won't be released. We are campaigning to raise awareness on the issue of consent. Each officer spied on hundreds of people. We want to highlight the scale of this huge anti-democratic scandal.

When the public hearings take place, we must mobilise people to attend and to write about it, report on it and raise awareness, so that others can realise they were impacted and come forward. This is the next stage of the campaign.

Despite everything that happened, I take positives from it. I have realised that there are many decent people out there who are a force for progressive change and who have provided support to me, and me to them. They have been brilliant and together we have taken the campaign forward. Individually we are weak – I don't know how I would have coped alone – but collectively we are strong and we have achieved a lot.

I have built resilience – taking on the state requires lots of resilience and determination. They will do anything to protect themselves. I don't want this to happen to anyone else. I must see it through. I want to be sure I have done all I can. I am so grateful that I have learned so much from so many brilliant activists.

These friendships matter a lot to me and the work we are doing is impressive – we want to build a better life for everyone. I have never stopped trusting people. In fact, this experience has made me so much stronger.

MARGARET ASPINALL

Justice for the 96

Margaret Aspinall's son James went to a football match at the Hillsborough stadium on 15 April 1989. Like 95 of his fellow Liverpool fans, he never came home. From that day to this, the families of the 96 have fought a battle for the truth.

Every step of the way, the Hillsborough families have been forced to fight very powerful forces. South Yorkshire Police, the justice system, the Thatcher Government, the football authorities and the Murdoch press all played their part in trying to suppress the truth about what happened that fateful day in Sheffield. But the Hillsborough families refused to be silenced. They refused to accept the version of events presented by those with a vested interest in maintaining the lies about Hillsborough. The Aspinall family's fight is the Hillsborough families' fight; the Hillsborough families' fight is all our fight.

I WAS BORN IN Huyton – now called Knowsley – one of ten children. My mum had five sons and five daughters. She was a very strict parent and made sure we were all law abiding. We never played out on the street or annoyed our neighbours. None of us gave our parents an ounce of trouble and we all went on to have jobs.

I went to St Agnes's Primary School, then on to high school, leaving at 15. There was no chance I would have stayed on, as we needed the money to contribute to the house. My first wage packet was £2 2s a week, as a machine operator in Huntley and Palmer's biscuit factory – I loved that job. My mum let me keep two shillings to myself from my wages and that bought me my lunch each day. Whatever was left I had to save for clothes and everything else. We all accepted this, as we knew how hard it was for our parents to provide for the ten of us.

My older sister worked in the bank, one of my brothers worked on a farm, two others on the railway. We didn't get the chance to be academic but we all knew right from wrong, that was drummed into us. My mum instilled into us that you had to fight for what you believe in, but you should never use physical violence.

My 'Nin' – that's was we called my grandmother – was staunch Labour. When Harold Wilson was the local MP in Huyton, he used a room in her house for meetings and when he became Prime Minister, he sent for Nin and recalled that time with her. Our family was staunch Labour, but I wasn't political in the party sense. I believed more in people doing right by me and I would do right by them. I worked in the factory until I got married at 23, then I went back to do evening shifts until the factory closed. I never really had another job. Huntley and Palmer employed over 1,000 at its peak. The people there worked hard – we only ever had one small strike. It was a contented workforce.

I had five of family; a couple are still in the house with me. I can't get rid of them, they keep coming back! James was 18 when Hillsborough happened. He worked with a shipping company in James Street at that time. David was 15, Kerry nine, Andrew seven and Louise six. My husband, Jim, was a big Liverpool supporter, as were the boys. I wasn't a football supporter. I didn't understand what they were all getting so excited about. Jimmy went to matches every week but we didn't have the money to send the boys every week. When James started working, he had a bit more money and would go to the matches. The game at Hillsborough was his first away game.

When I tell the story of that day, I try to pretend to myself that James was not part of it. I have always done that. It helps me cope. When I talk about James I always remember there were 95 others, it is not just about James. There are also so many survivors who still suffer to this day. So, it is not just about me and mine, but because I am chair of the Hillsborough Families Support Group, people ask about my son and I understand that, and I think the families do too.

On that particular day, my husband was going to the match with my brother-in-law and his brother and a friend. There was room for James in the car, but because he was going with his friend, Graham Wright, who also lost his life at Hillsborough, he wouldn't go in the car and leave Graham, so they went by coach.

He always liked to get home in time for *Neighbours* on TV. He was about 15 minutes late that day and when he got in he held up his match ticket and said, 'Ha, Mum, I'm 18 – you can't stop me going to away matches match now. I've got a ticket for the game.' And he waved it around.

I said, 'What game? The semi-final in Sheffield? I don't want you to go.'

'You can't stop me now, Mum.' He laughed and joked, showing everyone his ticket.

The next morning when he got up, he asked me to help him put on the gold chain I bought him for his 18th birthday. I said to him, 'Good God, James, if anything happens to me, what are you going to do – you'll have to learn to put this on yourself.'

He said, 'Don't say that, Mum... Right, that's me. I'm off to game.' And he turned around and said, 'Mum, what time is our Kez home today?'

Kez was the name he and our children gave their sister Kerry. James always looked after Kerry. Wherever they went, he always took her hand. She had gone away with her Auntie Rose and Uncle John to Cornwall for the week, so he hadn't seen her for seven days and he was missing her.

I said, 'I think they'll be home at about 12.'

He said, 'Mum, please let her stay up until I get back, don't do your usual and put her to bed at six o'clock. I will be back around seven o'clock so let her stay up so I can see her, I won't go to mass tonight I will go in the morning.'

I said, 'Okay, I'll let her stay up.'

So off he went to the match.

Rose and John came home with Kerry at about 12.30. She ran in, asking where James, David and the rest were.

I said, 'James is at the match but you can stay up to see him when he gets back.'

Kerry said excitedly, 'I've got him a present.' James had given her some money to spend on her break.

Unbeknown to me, she put James's present under his pillow in his bedroom – I only found this out later. Kerry went upstairs to see Louise, who was playing with her dolls in her room.

Rose and John sat down and put the TV on to try and catch up with the latest on the match. I went to make some sandwiches for lunch. All of a sudden, Rose shouted, 'Margaret there's something going on at Hillsborough at the football.'

I said, 'It's okay, James and Jimmy are not at Hillsborough, they are at Sheffield.' I didn't know Hillsborough was in Sheffield – that's how much I paid attention to football.

She said, 'Margaret, Hillsborough is Sheffield Wednesday, come and have a look on the telly.'

When I saw the screen, I saw people getting laid on the pitch. 'They've all fainted,' I said. 'They have all passed out.'

Then I heard the commentator say there had been seven fatalities.

'Oh my God, seven people are dead – is that definitely where Jimmy and James are?'

Rose said, 'Yes, it is!'

Then they gave out the emergency number to phone – I immediately tried it but couldn't get through. I wasn't even thinking of my husband at this point, I was only thinking about my child. All I could think was, he only went to see football and now all this has happened, what is going on?

Rose then said, 'It's more than seven, its going up and up.'

I screamed, 'Turn the telly off!'

I tried to get in touch with the coach company, Barnes Travel, but couldn't get through. In the meantime, my mum, dad, sisters and friends were calling. I urged them to stay off the phone to keep the line free – there were no mobiles then.

At around 6.30pm, my husband Jimmy called and asked, 'Have you heard from James?'

I said, 'Oh God, have you not seen him since the game?'

'No,' he replied.

I said, 'Please look for him and don't come home without him.' Poor Jimmy, he went through hell that day.

Jimmy said he would continue to call me regularly until he found James.

At around 7.45pm, I eventually got through to the bus company who said all the people who travelled were accounted for, but the coaches were being impounded and they won't be back in Liverpool until midnight.

Naturally, I thought he was safe. I told Rose and John, and Jimmy when he called. In the meantime, Jimmy had been at every hospital and back to the stadium but there was still no sign of James and Graham – I told him to come home as James was safe. He said, 'Thank Christ for that.'

Jimmy came home and we went down to Liverpool with a couple of James's friends. We waited until every coach came in. When the last one arrived and he never came off I went on and asked the driver, 'Where is he? Where is my son?'

He said, 'I'm sorry, all these people were just jumping on the coach to get home'.

I was annoyed, thinking someone had taken his seat and he had been left up there.

I said to Jimmy, 'You'll have to get back and find him. He could be walking around, traumatised.'

We then went to Truebrook Police Station and I said, 'My son was at Hillsborough, they have left him there and I don't know if he has any money or anything to get home. What do I do?'

The policeman said to me, 'We are waiting on a list coming through.'

I said, 'But he is not on any list – we have checked at the hospitals in Sheffield, he's not on their lists.'

He said, 'We are still waiting on the list. As soon as we get it we will be in touch, I can assure you of that.'

Jimmy told me to go home, saying, 'When he comes in he will need his mum, he will need a hug, so you go home and I will go up to Sheffield. I will call you regularly, if he comes home we can come straight back.'

When I got home the children were frantic. I tried to get them back to bed but they were crying and so was I.

Half an hour later, Jim called – no further news. Grandparents and friends and relatives called. I asked them to keep the line free. At around 4.00am, I stopped getting calls from Jimmy. I needed fresh air, so I went to take James's little dog for a walk, that must have been about 6.15am. I got out and looked up the road and saw my sister and her husband standing there, she had been crying. I said to myself, 'What is she doing there?' My husband came round the corner in the car. I couldn't see James. My worst memory is of my husband coming out of the car and James not being there. I started to run away. Jimmy shouted, 'Margaret! Margaret!'

I screamed back, 'Don't you dare catch up with me, don't you dare.'

My thought process was, if you catch me it's going to be true, if you don't catch me he's still alive. That was what I was thinking. I kept running and running. Someone said something, I turned around and saw my husband on the floor; I couldn't leave him like that… so I went back and said, 'Jimmy, where is he, where's James?'

Jimmy had a plastic bag with James's stuff. He gave me it. I said, 'I don't want his stuff, I want my son, please get him for me. I want him back.'

My mind was racing I started to think James had been punished by God for not going to mass last night – that was what was in my head – all these things were running through my mind. I saw his gold chain and his belt and his ID pass in the plastic bag. It had his picture and phone number and contact details – why hadn't they contacted us when they had his ID? Why had they put my family through torture? Why didn't they contact us?

I said to my husband, 'You know how James feels the cold, I need to put his coat on him, it's chilly.'

Poor Jimmy – we got in the car and went back to Sheffield again. We were sent to the Medical Legal Centre. When I walked in it was eerie – all I could hear was people sobbing and screaming. I thought, 'Why are they crying? They don't know James. Why are they all crying? They don't know my son.' I wasn't thinking about anyone else at this point. I gave my name to the Salvation Army people who were there helping, they were so good. They gave me a seat next to this lady and she put her arm around me. She said, 'Who have you lost?'

I said, 'I haven't lost anyone, he's here, I am taking him home.'

She sobbed, 'Okay dear, don't worry.'

Then a man came and said, 'Are you ready, Mrs Aspinall?'

'Ready for what?' I asked.

'Please come with us,' the man said.

I was taken into a room. It was horrible room.

The man said, 'Mrs Aspinall, we are going to pull the curtains back now. Are you ready?'

Jimmy said to me, 'Margaret, James is behind the screen.'

The curtains opened, and I screamed.

I sobbed, 'I want to hug him.'

The man said, 'I'm sorry, Mrs Aspinall, he now belongs to the coroner.'

I collapsed. I have no idea how I got out, I was probably carried out.

I was given a cup of tea and I said, 'I want to take him home with me in the car now. I want him to be with his family…'

I didn't get him back home until five days later, in a coffin.

Even then I wasn't allowed to touch him, the undertakers told us not to, on instruction from the coroner. All I wanted to do was hug and squeeze him, but we were denied that. I just wish I had had a few minutes before he passed away, just to tell him how much I loved him and how much I was proud of him.

I believe the people who were beside him were so fortunate and lucky to have been there, to have had the honour to be with my son at the end of his life. I was there when he had his first breath, but I was denied being there when he had his last, when he needed me, when he left this world.

My focus in the days following the death was on James and my family. My pain and grief were only for my family. I didn't think about the others at that time. That sound incredibly selfish, but it got me through those initial days.

We had a double funeral for James and Graham who was with him at the match. I don't remember a thing about the funeral. I have been told they had to put screens outside to relay the service to the crowds, but I don't remember any of it. It was all a blur. The only thing I can remember is the two coffins in church.

A few days later, a certain newspaper's headlines screamed about Hillsborough, blaming the Liverpool fans for their own deaths. My poor mum, James's gran, saw that and came to my house, she was in a terrible state. She said, 'This is going to be the death of me. They are trying to say the Liverpool fans were responsible.' She said to me, 'Do not buy any newspapers, that's not the only one reporting this.'

I said, 'I don't want to see the newspapers or the telly... I don't want to know what they are saying about it.'

A memorial service was arranged four weeks later at the Anglican cathedral. I didn't want to go but the family wanted me to – they all said, 'You must go for James.'

So, I went and when we got there, the families of the victims were all shoved to back. The seats at the front were all reserved for the 'dignitaries'. We weren't the dignitaries, we were just the losers. Then of course Mrs Thatcher came in (I am being respectful here, as I do not want to say what I really think of her), she came in with an entourage.

I turned and said to Jim, 'What are we doing here? My son is over the road in a grave. Why am I here?' He urged me to stay.

After the service, one of the men from the church came over to the families and said, 'We would like you all to go down to the crypt, Mrs Thatcher would like to meet all of the families there.'

Now I am not ashamed to say this, I don't care what people think of me, I said to Jimmy, 'I don't want to go down to the crypt.'

Again, the family cajoled me into going. I went to avoid any arguments.

In the crypt it was all very regimented. I said to Jimmy, 'This reminds me of bloody Butlin's where you all get lined up and almost forced to take part in some game or something or other.'

Mrs Thatcher and Douglas Hurd, the Home Secretary, came in and were shaking hands with family members and having a little chat.

I said to Jimmy, 'The one thing I am not doing is shaking her hand... don't even ask me to. I will not shake her hand until I get the truth of what happened.'

She came along and shook Jimmy's hand – I was fuming with him for doing that, I didn't half tell him when we got outside.

She came to me and I said, 'I'm sorry, Mrs Thatcher, I do not want to shake your hand just now.'

'Why ever not, dear?' she said in that voice.

I said, 'Until you can tell me the truth about what happened to my son who is buried over the road, my son dead having attended his first ever away game, then I won't shake your hand. When you give me truth of what happened, I will willingly shake your hand, not before.'

She said, 'My dear, there were 750 policemen on duty that day...'

I said, 'Wrong! Get you facts right, Mrs Thatcher, there were a lot more than that.' I was pointing my finger at her and I said, 'Will you tell me what the hell they were doing that day?'

'Their job, my dear, their job... I'd better step away from you, dear, you are so angry.'

I said, 'I will do you a favour, Mrs Thatcher, I will walk away from you.' And I walked out.

I wasn't ashamed of myself for that, I was very proud of myself for what I had said and done. Her hand wasn't good enough to be shaken by the mother of James Aspinall. That is how I looked at it. I told Jimmy to wash his hand and I told him we now had a fight on our hands to expose the truth of what happened to those innocent people. That is when I got strong. I realised this was not just about the fans who died, the survivors and families it was about our city. It was about us, Liverpool and its people. My son gave me the strength that day.

After the events of Hillsborough, a group of social workers started working with the families. One of them, Antoinette, told me about a lovely woman called Joan Traynor who lost two sons at Hillsborough – she and Bill Pemberton were trying to get in touch with all the families to bring them together. Antoinette passed on our details. Between the social workers and some of the families, people were brought together. There was a big meeting and I am so glad I went. I was so pleased to see I was not alone.

At that meeting, I realised that they loved the people they lost just as much as I loved James. Before that, I had it in my head that no one could possibly love their child or relative as much as I did. I now knew differently. Each one of them was loved just as much as James was. That helped me greatly.

It took a few meetings to get ourselves organised. We formed a committee, some of whom, sadly, have since died. I was one of the quieter ones who joined not as an office bearer, just a member of the group. We raised funds to get us going and started to get to work. I learned so much from the families and those who came forward, they were great mentors. They taught me how to deal with the press, how to lobby and pressure the government. I quickly realised that too many voices is sometimes not effective when you are having meetings. So, we established an executive committee to bring focus, especially when meeting with government and officials, lawyers, politicians, etc. They are more likely to listen to a few, strong, representative voices who know the issues than to a big group raising lots of different issues at the same time.

Every stage of the process was a learning curve. Governments often leave people thinking they are getting something when in reality they aren't, you can easily fall for it.

We were told in the early days that you had to go through all the stages in the British legal system before you could go to the European Courts. But we went through every stage and still got the door slammed in our faces by the EU.

When you go back to the beginning, we had a mini-inquest to find out how they died and where they died – well, we bloody knew this already. What we wanted to know was why they died. The mini-inquest gave us an interim death certificate to allow us to bury our sons and daughters. You go along to that and ask a few questions, you are then told you will get the answers to your questions at the generic inquest.

Then we had the Taylor Report. Many people were happy with Taylor, and yes, he did a decent job, but there was so much more he knew and so much more he could have done. However, I think a lot was glossed over and many witnesses weren't spoken to. We then had the generic inquest. Well, we didn't get any answers there either, all we got was bloody lies. For 30 years we have been told to keep our mouths closed. All though judicial reviews, the private prosecutions, the scrutiny and so on. Year after year after year, we didn't get the answers we needed. We needed a breakthrough, but we were constantly being let down.

In 2009/10 I took over as chair of the Hillsborough Families Support Group. Up until that time we had never allowed an MP to speak at our annual memorial service. The families never trusted MPs and wouldn't allow it. Now I am not ashamed to say this, but I made a decision I shouldn't have. Let me explain. Andy Burnham, Steve Rotherham and Maria Eagle had been supportive of our campaign, so I spoke to Andy and as the memorial service drew closer, he and Steve Rotherham got in touch to say that they had a letter from the Prime Minister, Gordon Brown, that they wanted to read out at the memorial service. Andy asked me if I would read it out. I let it run through my mind and thought deeply about it, but I was so frustrated that we were getting nowhere. I thought, what the hell, what the hell? I felt that Andy should speak at the service. I knew if the committee found out they would not allow it, so I took the decision on my own. Andy was very nervous. When I told one or two of the committee members, they weren't at all happy and said, 'You better tell him it's not on, the families will lynch you.'

I said, 'Sorry, I have made that decision – if it goes wrong I will resign but I am sticking with it. You won't be held responsible, I will take full responsibility.'

On the day, Andy came into the back room, very anxious. I said, 'Look, you are going to get stick – but take it.'

He gave me a big hug and said, 'Let's do it.'

He stood up to read the letter and as he did the fans spontaneously started chanting 'Justice for the 96! Justice for the 96!' On and on they went. 'Justice for the 96! Justice for the 96.' Again and again they sang it. And Andy looked out into the crowd and he took it.

One of the committee members asked me, 'Do you want me to try to stop the crowd?'

I said, 'No... leave it, let him take it.'

That was a one of the best decisions I have ever made. Afterwards, Andy said, 'Margaret, I promise you... something has to be done about this... I will take this message back to the Prime Minister, something has to be done.'

I looked him in the eye and said, 'Do not let me down!'

Within a few weeks, I was receiving phone calls from the Ministry of Justice. Our executive committee met with the Home Secretary, we met with civil servants, we got the Hillsborough Independent Panel established and were instrumental in drawing up the terms of reference for it. We got the right people on the panel, we met with them and had a belief they would do a good job. The panel undertook its work – Bishop Jones, the chair of the HIP, published his report and launched it at the Anglican cathedral. The panel reported it has discovered new and very important information. Despite a change of government at the general election, progress continued. Attorney General Dominic Grieve overturned the inquest verdicts. Then there were the new inquests. I went to meet with Theresa May several times. I asked for funding to allow us to be properly represented, as we had no funding and all of the other agencies has always been fully funded. Credit where credit is due, Theresa May helped us in many different ways. Undoubtedly the HIP's work was a real turning point.

So, we got the new inquests, it took two years to do them all and they concluded that in 95 cases the verdict was unlawful killing. In poor Tony Bland's case, because he died a year later, they couldn't give that verdict, which is disgrace, in my view.

Then we had the trial of the police match commander on the day, Mr Duckenfield. The trial failed to reach a verdict, then at retrial he was found not guilty. The safety officer at Sheffield Wednesday was found guilty and fined £6,000 – £6,000, what a bloody insult.

So we will have to go through all of this again with the trial of another five officers for the cover up. It still goes on and on.

From all of this I have learned that when you have a cause that is just, when you know things have happened that shouldn't have, then stick with it. There will be days when you think you cannot go on, when you are tired and want it to end, but that is what they want. They want you to get tired and fed up and feel you can't do anymore. When this happens, go back to the reason why you started out in the first place. Make them sick of you, rather than you sick of them. Never ever give up – not matter how many knockbacks, come back more determined than ever. When you feel weak, be inspired by the people and cause you care about. We can't do these things on our own, we get our strength from each other.

I have met powerful people and celebrities, but I tell you it's the ordinary people who mean more to me. They are the ones who keep you going. I only met these famous people because 96 people died – I didn't want to meet them.

I said to the families and fans at one of our anniversary services, 'We are the eyes of the 96, we are the ears of the 96 and most importantly we are the voices of the 96.' That is what it is about – we are doing this for the good of the people, the good of the nation. We may have a stronger voice than some, but we are buoyed by the ordinary people who support us, who don't have a voice.

I'll leave you with this – one day I was walking through Liverpool and I saw a homeless guy sitting in the street on a bit of cardboard in the pouring rain. I opened my purse and gave him two-pound coins. He got up and ran after us. I thought he wanted more money but no he had recognised me from the campaign.

He said, 'I can't take that from you. Please put that money to Hillsborough fund.'

I told him, 'I won't take it back, you need it.' We had little argument about who needed the money most.

Then I said, 'Look you take a pound and I will take a pound, and we had a hug'. I kept that pound, I still have it. I will keep it and treasure it. That pound from that homeless man is like getting a million pounds from someone who has plenty. That is how good and generous the ordinary people are.

I'm looking forward to the future. My children and grandchildren have learned a lot through all of this. I always tell them: 'No one is better than you, but you are no better than them.' That is important. I told the MPs and Lords in the Houses of Parliament this when I spoke to them recently. I told them that they were no better than the people walking around outside. That jobs and clothes and wealth don't make a man or a woman. It's what's inside that matters. It's what's in your heart that matters.

Some people believe the families got a lot of money when our sons and daughters and family members died. Let me tell you we got £1,250 of an insurance payment for our son's life – we had to use that to pay towards the £3,500 we needed to be represented by a lawyer at the inquest. What a disgrace. I told the MPs and Lords all of that. That is how the system treated the Hillsborough families. But as I said, we did get a breakthrough and now the truth is out there. On 12 September 2016, the Hillsborough Independent Panel reported its findings. We stood on the steps of St George's hall in Liverpool and the truth came out.

In May 2021, two retired police officers and an ex-solicitor accused of altering police statements after the Hillsborough disaster were acquitted by the courts. The Hillsborough families' pursuit of justice continues.

YVETTE WILLIAMS

Grenfell

Yvette Williams is the daughter of an Antiguan migrant who came to the UK in the 1950s. Heavily influenced by her community activist father and the social and economic conditions experienced by the black community in Birmingham and London she became active in community organisations fighting for justice and equality. As a London resident, she lives near Grenfell Tower and was there on the night of the fire, which claimed at least 72 lives. In the immediate aftermath of the fire it was left to the community to respond to the tragedy as the local council and central government was posted missing. In the following weeks, Yvette worked in a voluntary capacity, using extensive networks built up over the years to help provide support and practical advice to bereaved families and those left homeless. Later, she co-founded the Justice for Grenfell campaign.

I WAS BROUGHT up in Birmingham after my parents moved to the UK from Antigua, famous for being the home of the great Viv Richards; cricket is one of my loves. They came here is the mid-'50s and were pretty young at the time, in their very early 20s. My dad came first with four friends, one of them had links to people in Birmingham. They came partly for economic reasons but also to advance their education. They planned to get a job in London first to raise some money before going on to study; one already had a place at Art College. One member of the group was Kelso Cochrane, who was murdered in Notting Hill in London in 1959 in a racist attack that was a precursor to the Notting Hill riots. This all happened at the time when Oswald Mosley was around. My dad never got over the death of his friend, he was shattered by it.

We ended up living in Saltley, Birmingham, which became famous for the 'Battle of Saltley Gate' (the media description of clashes that took place during the mass picketing of a fuel storage depot). My dad worked with British Rail during the 1970s at the time of power cuts and the three-day week under Heath. I did not really know why coal and miners were anything to do with my dad, a railway worker; I just knew that on certain days he would say that he was on strike. I started to get an idea from him, and from my mum, about what was right, and what was wrong. They were, I suppose, instilling union ethics in me early.

Around this time, there was significant activity in Birmingham by the National Front. My dad was very involved in the counter to that. Our house was a community house and he was viewed as a stalwart of that community. People would come to him for advice on finances, paperwork and the like; he also set up a youth club. Stop and search was a big issue then and he helped get legal advice for parents of kids caught up in this.

In the late '70s, 'Rock Against Racism' was huge in Birmingham and while we all went out and had a good time listening to the bands, many of us were also politicised by the speeches and what we heard in between the acts. I got increasingly involved in our local community centre activities. During the holidays, I would return to London and Notting Hill as my godfather lived there.

I wanted to go to university, broaden my horizons and get out of Birmingham. In the year I left school, 1981, me and three friends bunked off school to go to a demonstration about The New Cross fire, where over 13 people died at party after a suspected fire-bombing by far-right extremists. No one has ever been held to account for these deaths.

I then moved to Notting Hill, got involved in a number of issues, and went to a lot of public meetings and events. I got involved with The Mangrove, a restaurant set up by Frank Crichlow, a Trinidadian community rights activist –a gathering point for the Caribbean community. It was a very political place and came in for a lot of police attention. It was raided on many occasions and people were arrested. Following a raid in 1970, there was protest where nine black activists were arrested and charged for alleged incitement to riot. They became known as the Mangrove Nine. Following a 55-day trial at the Old Bailey, all were acquitted of this charge. The trial became the first judicial acknowledgement of behaviour motivated by racial hatred with in the Metropolitan Police. Out of that came the Mangrove Trust and Mangrove Community Association. We were pushing the race equalities agenda and helped set up conferences and events, as well as assisting the community with housing, education and legal issues they were facing. We joined together with other voluntary groups. Following a conference in Nottingham, the National Black Caucus was set up, with its London headquarters at The Mangrove. I was a student all through this period at Goldsmiths and got involved in many different issues.

Frank Crichlow was arrested on drugs charges, put under curfew and couldn't work in his restaurant, which eventually had to close (the trust kept going). They wanted rid of Frank and went for him in a big way. It was awful because many organisations such as an anti-apartheid group, Cuba Solidarity and others used The Mangrove for meetings, discussion and organising, but now they had to move elsewhere.

I became involved in the Labour Party around 1985/86. About this time, we did an event called Focus '86. We were worried that the conditions were right for further race riots and unrest in our communities. Two of the keynote speakers at this meeting were Diane Abbot, who was a Westminster councillor at that time, and Paul Boateng. Both were trying to become parliamentary candidates, so we organised for them and some of our other black colleagues who were trying to become councillors to share a platform. We worked very closely with the Labour Party in London and often attended Labour Black Section meetings – especially those led by the late Bernie Grant, who gave the Mangrove a lot of support. We also had great union support from people like Bill Morris, Manny Blake, Bob Purkiss, Gloria Mills and Harriet Harman. We continued our work and went on mounting events and organising on black women's issues, housing, educational attainment, crime and justice, employment, youth – all sorts of things. We started to make real progress in terms of representation and racial equality with the election of Diane, Paul, Bernie and Keith in 1987. In response to growing community concern about racism, deportations and increasing racial violence and murders, we became involved in the Anti-Racist Alliance when it was established in 1991, chaired by Marc Wadsworth and then Ken Livingstone.

In 1993, Derek Beacon was elected in Tower Hamlets, the first BNP councillor anywhere in the UK. There followed a string of racist attacks and violence, racist graffiti and abuse, in and around Lewisham. Two men, Quddus Ali and Mukhtar Ahmed, were very badly beaten. There was another high-profile murder and the atmosphere was one of fear and violence. Following these attacks, we had the murders of Roland Adams and Stephen Lawrence within a short space of time. We worked closely with these campaigns and looked at how we could advance equality and challenge racism and discrimination in the community.

I'm a founding member of Operation Black Vote, established in 1996. Jack Straw was Shadow Home Secretary at the time and committed that if a Labour government was elected in the 1997 election, he would commit to an inquiry into the Lawrence case. We aimed to mobilise the black community to participate in the upcoming election and worked to ensure black people across the country registered to vote.

This was a bad time for me, as my dad died and by the time I sorted his estate, I had qualified as a teacher and was doing some part-time agency work. I attended some of the Lawrence Inquiry as a volunteer.

Dr Richard Stone was a Lawrence Inquiry panel member. We knew and trusted Richard. He was a GP in Notting Hill and we often called on him to attend the local police station to record the injuries of those who had been beaten up in custody. He went on to be one of the main funders of the Mangrove Trust. We developed a mantra of Black self-reliance from 'cradle to grave' and set up a care home for our elders, a women's ex-offenders' hostel, a drug rehabilitation project and community events.

When the MacPherson Report came out, I was encouraged to apply for a job in the civil service to help write much needed hate crime prosecution policies and community engagement strategies. I also looked at equality and diversity in employment. I was there for 15 years, during which time I also sat on some community boards and helped with campaigns. When I left the CPS, I pottered about in campaigns on a number of local issues, until 14 June 2017, when I found myself standing at the bottom of Grenfell Tower as it was engulfed in flames.

On the evening of the Grenfell fire I was at home. Nothing much was happening, it was an ordinary summer night. I live near the tower, within walking distance. My phone rang and I saw it was a friend, but as it was the early hours of the morning, I left it as I did not really want to speak to someone at that time. Fortunately, she had my landline and I picked up to hear her say she had been evacuated from her home because 'Moroccan Tower' was on fire. She lived in one of the walkways under the tower. ('Moroccan Tower was how it was referred to locally, because in the late '70s and early '80sw many Moroccan families lived there.)

I tried to drive down to the tower but could not get far, so I got out and walked. This was around 1.30am. The fire at this point looked contained; while it was alarming, it wasn't at this point out of control.

Just as I found my friend, we heard a huge whooshing noise, almost like gas exploding. People were stunned and horrified by what they were seeing. From where I was, we could see people at windows. I never saw anyone jump but I knew not everyone would come out alive; I feared the numbers of fatalities would be high.

The streets at this point were not full of people, but more and more came as the night went on. I don't think many people knew it was happening as they were in bed. Okay, there was a police helicopter overhead, but we are used to that here – people would have just thought it was the police looking for someone. If no one phoned, you during the night, you would only have known in the morning when you switched on your phone or the TV or radio or went outside.

At 5.17am, I posted on my social media, 'Inshallah, our Muslim brothers have come with water'. They were the first people who came with help and it was water. They had been at mosque during Ramadan and had gathered up bottled water. I saw no one from the authorities there at this time, there was nothing for people and the community had to respond as best we could. In the morning, I asked my daughter if she wanted to go to school and she did, and then found out that one her friends was missing. On the way back, I went into see a local vicar who agreed to set up a local donation centre in Latimer Road. In the streets, we spontaneously phoned people we knew, alerted friends we knew, tried to list people we knew who were missing, looked after people who came out. People just helped by doing what they could.

The Latimer Christian Centre opened up a relief centre where I helped and then at around 11.00am a community activist told me he had keys to an empty unit, so we moved in there and worked from it for the next few days, taking and sorting donations generously given by the public.

In the run-up to the fire, local resentment to the council and authorities had been growing. People knew for a long time about the shoddy and shabby refurbishment of the tower. People knew the cheap cladding went up so that the look of the tower wouldn't offend the eyes of the millionaires who had to see it from the windows of their big houses, or shoppers on the way to Westfield Shopping Centre. Many of us are convinced they were going to demolish the tower because of its condition, but instead did a cheap cosmetic job as a stopgap to paper over the cracks. A local estate had been what they called 'regenerated'; we called it 'gentrification'. The local authority moved all the residents out during this time, on the promise that they would return. Only 25 per cent of the tenants were rehoused back on the estate. They built lovely million-pound townhouses that they sold off. Of course, no one in the community could afford them or even dream of affording them. Many of the previous tenants were moved out of the borough never to return, some out of

London altogether.

They were just about to do the same thing on the Silchester estate (opposite the estate where Grenfell tower stands). The local authority had over years carried out a policy of 'managed decline' of the properties to justify their actions. They failed to respond to repairs requests and when the damage hit rock bottom, they said, 'Well these houses are in such a poor condition, it's not worth repairing and we can offer you a flat in Peterborough or Lincoln or somewhere else, you cannot go back there.' We saw it as form of 'class cleansing' of the area and gerrymandering of the borough – driving our working-class people out to make way for new expensive housing for the rich.

They also shut down the council play service to save £750,000 – we suggested they sell the Lord Mayor's jewels, or take away his chauffeur, or cut their wine bill to help pay for it – of course, they refused. They closed a valued nursery, they threatened to close the library and attempted to sell off the local further education college. They privatised services, claiming it would save money; the companies who came in were left to get on with it with no accountability to the public they were supposed to serve. At this time, the council had reserves of £274 million – their latest accounts show they still have a high level of reserves in the bank, despite claims they are broke. It also looks like the houses they have now purchased to try and house survivors may not have been bought with any council cash but were only bought only because of central government grants that eventually came through.

A local organisation called the West Way 23 was looking at how the council was treating the working-class end of the borough. It was originally looking at how the community could get back the 23 acres of land under the West Way, land which had previously been given to the community but was now being taken back by the council.

On so many fronts, they were taking from the poor to give to the wealthy residents, who they saw as their supporters. We used the term 'institutional indifference' to explain what was going on. They didn't hate us, they just didn't give a toss about us!

On the Thursday before the fire, the general election took place. The count is usually completed on the Friday in the early hours of the morning but ours took three counts and the result came in late on the Friday night, when for the first time we elected a Labour MP, Emma Dent Coad, by a majority of 20 votes. This was without doubt part of the reaction to the appalling treatment of communities in the borough.

In terms of the fire itself, at least 72 people died. They came from a wide variety of nationalities, ethnicities, and religions – the tower's residents accurately reflected the historic demography of the area. We had the white English working class, Irish, Spanish, Portuguese, African Caribbean, Moroccan, Lebanese, Iranian, Eritrean, and Ethiopian and more. We also had 14 people who had bought their flats and leaseholders.

The campaign came together on about the 18th of June, when a local guy, Ishmahil, who had been doing some good interviews on the media and social media and I spoke about setting up a campaign. We wanted to avoid the authorities coming in, buying off a few influential people and doing the usual divide and conquer tactic. During this period, some people had gone to the town hall and tried to kick the door in. We understood this, but we wanted to bring some calm and focus to people's anger. On the Sunday, we held a meeting and the idea for a silent walk was proposed. This helped remove some of the rising tension and give people some thinking space. We got a lot of community people to speak from the platform calling for unity and people to think carefully about the tasks ahead. We also got Michael Mansfield QC to come to explain about how an inquiry and inquest would work and other legal matters.

For the next few days, we worked out of Ishmahil's basement, where we had a number of bereaved families coming in (the council did not even have an accurate list of tenants). We became a bit of an advice centre, helping people get lawyers and pointing them in the direction of support. All of this was voluntary at this stage. We also used our networks of supporters who could assist.

In the meantime, we brought together the bereaved families for a closed meeting to allow them to get to know each other and build relationships – that had not happened up until this point. It was all very informal, reactive and organic for the next three or four months. We were simply trying to help the bereaved and now homeless residents cope with visa extensions, housing, funerals, etc. In the area, there was a bit of counter movement claiming Grenfell was not political – we knew it was hugely political.

Then the inquiry chair was appointed in August (Sir Martin Moore-Bick). They said they would consult with the community about that appointment but did not. We wanted someone who understood the community and pointed to the Lawrence Inquiry Panel as a good model of how to do things, but they ignored that. Then they tried to cut down on the people who would be core participants. Victims and families were not being housed with any urgency, we even had to demand that information go out in community languages – basic stuff. All the while, the leader and deputy leader of the council were still waltzing around footloose and fancy free – they have since resigned because of the pressure the community brought upon them, not through any feeling that they were accountable.

With inquiry proceeding, we had to formalise things in the campaign. The MP managed to secure offices for us to use free. Trade unions like UNITE, FBU,

PCS, GMB, ASLEF and RMT helped us with furniture, computers and banners. One of the charitable trusts supported an application for cash.

We did not really know what we were doing but we knew we could call on people to help and guide use, so we set up an advisory board to do that. These were people we could pick up the phone to and say, 'Where do you think we should be going with this?' and they would offer wise guidance. We do not take the credit for any of this; we were just blessed to have good networks that we knew we could rely on.

At the beginning, we wanted all publicly donated money to go to the bereaved and survivors. The campaign's biggest funders initially were the unions, who would do fundraisers for the cause and send a few thousand here and a few thousand there, which was great. Now we have website, we make it clear that donations are for our work, which is focused on the long-term goal of obtaining justice for the bereaved families, survivors, evacuated residents and the local community, while partnering with representative organisations. We are very clear on that. If people want to give directly to the bereaved and survivors, then there are other avenues for doing that.

With regards to housing survivors, they had to say whether they wanted to be rehoused in the borough or outside of it and around 50 per cent opted to be rehoused away from the area – quite a few went to Brent and Ealing. Of those who remain, a number just want to be left alone and get on with their lives.

There are still outstanding rehousing issues. Some people who haven't been rehoused yet are being regarded by the authorities as troublemakers, but they aren't. I know of one person who refused a property because it was on the same floor level as his previous house and they couldn't confirm to him that the cladding on the block was safe. This is hardly being a troublemaker; his concerns are totally justified. He is troubled, not troublesome.

We support everyone who approaches us and we try to build broad inclusive alliances to take forward our agenda.

The inquiry is ongoing but is being viewed as a farce by local people. We can all see the direction it is going in: they want to make the Fire Brigade the scapegoat for everything. Survivors gave evidence in phase one and described what happened on the night. Phase two will be the lead up to and the response to the fire.

We fear that Fire Brigade will be hung out to dry, without anyone taking responsibility for the cuts to the service that affected their ability to respond – fewer fire-fighters, closed stations, reduced fire pumps, poor communications equipment, etc. We think they will try to get the idea of the Fire Service being to blame into the public psyche so that everything else, all the political decision-making that impacted on events will be secondary.

On the 14th of each month, we attend a silent walk of remembrance and respect where we walk from the Methodist Church to the 'Wall of Truth' which emerged as a gathering point after the fire. It holds photographs, tributes poems and other things relating to victims. Some of the fire-fighters and union branches join us and similar events happen across the country – Liverpool has a silent walk every month and other with towns and cities mark the event, especially on the anniversary.

Looking forward, Boris Johnson hasn't mentioned Grenfell since he became Prime Minister. We want to build a broader movement to bring in justice campaigns like Aberfan, Hillsborough and others to work together so we can hold the state to account and force change. The idea is to get people to act local and think national – challenge the lack of accountability, the role of establishment in holding down working people, asking: whose lives matter? We are raising questions about privatisation of future of public services and the impact on our communities. This is what is driving us.

We have the monthly silent walk – but our campaign is not about staying silent, People often stay silent because they think they are alone. But if not you, who? Some fear they may not know what they are doing, but this can be strength because people with great ideas come forward, ideas that people like me would never think of. One of the most effective was driving the 'three billboards outside Grenfell' trailer through the streets of London and this captured the imagination, raised awareness and kept this issue of Grenfell in the public consciousness. We have used the skills of the community, especially using creative energy via social media, music and communications to get out the message. People should not be afraid to offer their views and ideas. Young people help us get through to a new audience via music, culture and taking an open and inclusive approach. Knowing the people who can help and who mutually support each other is vital in such a campaign. We have seen real mutual intergenerational learning, but what has gone before us has had a huge influence and has given us a tremendous grounding for establishing and organising the campaign Justice for Grenfell.

The Public Inquiry into Grenfell is ongoing.

Mesh

Elaine Holmes and Olive McIlroy are my heroes. These two women from the west of Scotland came together in 2011 after finding each other by chance. Both were suffering badly from severe pain and disability following so-called 'routine' surgery to treat incontinence.

They went on to form the Scottish Mesh survivors' Hear Our Voice campaign and helped bring the transvaginal mesh scandal to national and international consciousness as one of the great global health scandals of our time, with hundreds of thousands of women across the globe affected.

The mesh story (or scandal) lays bare how multinational medical products manufacturers, working hand-in-glove with the corporate establishment, health regulators and other vested interests, have ignored the health and well-being of patients to protect profits and their own professional self-interest.

Elaine and Olive, along with the rest of the heroic Scottish mesh survivors, have taken on powerful figures and organisations such as the Scottish Government, the MHRA and regulators with determination, skill, dignity and honour, and in doing so have helped prevent many more women from going through the agony they have.

They are just two of an army of women across the globe whose lives have been devastated by mesh but whose resolve to fight for justice and improved care for victims burns brighter than ever.

OLIVE – I was born in Barshaw Park Hospital in Paisley. I am the oldest of a family of eight. My granny used to say she was frightened to look at my mum sideways in case she was pregnant again!

We stayed in a tenement building in Abercorn Street in a three-apartment flat, four floors up. My family stayed in number 86, my granny stayed in number 80 and my aunty at number 88. I stayed with granny most of the time because there was bedlam with so many of us in a small flat. But it was a happy bedlam.

We then moved to a five-apartment in Gallowhill in Paisley. It was like moving into a palace. I got a room to myself, which was amazing. I went to Abercorn Primary School then Oakshaw High. My mum worked as a cleaner in the NHS, one of the many jobs she had over the years. My dad had various jobs too, including at the Chrysler car factory in Linwood.

I left school when I was 15 and went to work in Woolworths on Paisley High Street for a year before going to Playtex in Johnstone for five years as a sewing machinist.

I got married in 1977 to my husband, Tommy. Our daughter was born in 1983 and our son in 1989. I went on to work in a laboratory bottling liquids used in hospitals and had a spell as a childminder before working for Tesco.

In 2006, I had bilateral surgery for carpal tunnel syndrome and was part medically retired, but I managed to get back into work with a sports coaching company. My last job was in home care.

All my working life, I took jobs that allowed me to work around looking after our children. My husband worked at Babcock's, Renfrew, for over 45 years. He is now retired.

After my second child, I suffered from what doctors call stress urinary incontinence. I can't say for certain what caused the incontinence. It went on for years, but when I found myself dealing with clients suffering similar issues I decided to do something about it. I was referred by my GP to a gynaecologist, who told me that the best thing would be an operation to insert what he referred to as 'a tape' – a tape that would change my life. That is how he described it. He said I would be out of hospital in a day and back to work in a week or so, with no more incontinence.

I saw him as an expert in his field of medicine. He was an NHS doctor and

I believed and trusted him. Prior to the operation, I was concerned about taking time off work, but although physiotherapy helped it didn't make the improvements needed, so I went ahead with the operation. I strongly believe the offer of physiotherapy would not have been forthcoming if I had not mentioned my concerns about being off work too long.

ELAINE – I was born in 1964 in Maryhill in Glasgow. My family emigrated to Australia when I was four through the assisted passage scheme, which was intended to increase the country's population and to supply skilled workers necessary for the booming industries – we were known as the '£10 Poms'. The move didn't work out for us and when I was eight, my mum, my wee brother and I returned home to Maryhill.

I went to Gilshochill (Gilshie) Primary School, then North Kelvinside (NK) High School, as did my husband Jeff. When I was 15, my brother, John, who was 12 at the time, was killed by a bus. It was the worst time of our lives – an awful tragedy.

I lost interest in school after John's death and left in fourth year, when I was 16. I worked with British Telecom as an international telephone operator, on a big, old-fashioned, cord switchboard, which I enjoyed. I stayed with BT until I had my son, Derek. Four years later, my family was complete when our daughter, Carey, was born.

I did voluntary work with Oxfam during school hours, which I thoroughly enjoyed, so much so that I ended up managing two of their charity shops, full-time. My passion is researching our family history and I furthered my knowledge of this at Strathclyde University, where I was also introduced to Forensic Psychology.

During a routine smear test, a nurse advised me that I had a prolapsed bladder. I had known something was wrong: it had been most noticeable when Jeff and I were on a walking holiday on the beautiful Island of Colonsay (my favourite place in the whole world) – and I had to keep stopping to pee in the bushes.

My GP referred me to a gynaecologist, who advised that I had stress urinary and urge incontinence. My condition at that time was not horrendous, it was a nuisance more than anything – I had a bladder that leaked when I laughed or sneezed. I wanted to get it resolved.

I was advised to have a number of procedures all at once. The prolapse repair would involve lifting my bladder back to its proper position, securing it with stitches and trimming any excess tissue – 'hitch and stitch', as it's commonly known. The doctor also advised me to have a 'wee tape inserted', which would act like a sling under my urethra (water pipe), to help stop the leakage. I remember saying to him, 'You have overwhelmed me. I thought I was only coming here for a consultation and I'm not sure I'm ready for surgery. What about physiotherapy?'

He said, 'Physio won't work.' Nevertheless, I wanted to try it. He agreed with the words, 'Okay, but I'm sure I will soon see you back here for surgery.'

I worked hard with the specialist gynaecological physiotherapist and took her advice seriously, as I wanted to resolve things without surgery if possible. After six weeks of pelvic floor muscle strengthening exercises and bladder retraining, I noticed a significant improvement. I had better control of my bladder and wasn't constantly rushing to the loo.

OLIVE – My procedure was carried out at the Southern General Hospital in Glasgow. Thinking back on it, I knew very little about what they were going to do to me other than 'insert a tape'. I had asked about complications, but the doctor said not to worry, he had done hundreds of these operations. I was desperate for help, so I went along with it. I was told it would be a 20-minute procedure and that it was 'the new gold standard procedure'. I was a day case patient but stayed in overnight. I awoke to horrendous pain and complained about it, but the doctor said not to worry, it would go away as the effects of surgery wore off. My symptoms just got worse and worse. I went back to work but was suffering badly. The symptoms escalated in 2010 to the point I was peeing blood for days because of infection. The surgeon told me I would have some occasional pain, but to just get on with things and go back to work. I tried, but only lasted six months because the pain was so bad. I was told: 'This had never happened before. I don't know what your problems are, no one else is complaining. It's nothing to do with your procedure.'

I was off work for long periods of time and threatened with losing my job because I was struggling to do the tasks. Eventually I took voluntary redundancy and I have been on benefits ever since.

ELAINE – While physiotherapy improved my incontinence, I still had a bladder prolapse. My surgeon said he would repair it, as described earlier and strongly recommended fitting the 'wee tape' at the same time to avoid the need for two surgeries, two general anaesthetics and two periods of recovery. He said I'd be a 'new woman'. I trusted him and his professional judgement and agreed to go ahead.

I went for surgery and was told I would be in overnight but ended up in hospital for seven days. When I awoke after surgery the pain was horrendous. I could only lie on my right side, I couldn't pee, I couldn't sit as it felt as though I had been guillotined in my most intimate area and when I tried to walk, my legs gave way.

In the mornings when my surgeon did his rounds he would jokingly say 'Oh, oh, here's trouble.'

I asked him why I had so much pain and he replied, 'Well you've just had surgery and you will get pain.' But I knew this level of pain was not normal. It was terrible.

I was given antibiotics to treat an infection, opiate injections and medication for pain relief, had several different catheters inserted to empty my bladder because I couldn't pee and I developed high blood pressure, which I never had beforehand. I was bedridden and vulnerable. Four weeks after discharge, I was readmitted to the ward from A&E. The surgeon took me back to theatre to examine me under anaesthetic, then said he was happy with everything and the 'tape' was in the right place, where it should be.

Nine weeks post-op, despite having been given syringes containing local anaesthetic to numb my nether regions, copious amounts of meds for pain relief, more antibiotics to treat infections and anti-sickness drugs, I could not stand the pain anymore and completely broke down in my GP's surgery. Thank God, I had supportive GPs at Elmwood Medical Practice who believed me. My GP was not happy at the amount of times I had been passed from pillar to post, back and forth to the hospital since my surgery. He did not agree that my suffering was part of the normal healing process. He phoned the hospital while we were there and lost the rag with a junior doctor who clearly didn't understand the severity of my situation. He told them I'd had multiple hospital admissions in recent weeks and was on my way to A&E now, and that I needed help *now*. Rather than wait for an ambulance, Jeff helped me into the car and we headed for the hospital. I felt every bump on the road and cried in pain.

Jeff pushed me in a wheelchair to the ward. I couldn't stand without support and couldn't manage to get into a hospital bed. That was the day I completely lost my dignity. I stood in the middle of the ward, all eyes on me as a nurse went down on her hands and knees underneath me to remove my catheter. I screamed the place down as blood and pus poured all over the floor. She was shocked and the other patients were fearful that this might happen to them.

Soon afterwards, I was examined by a surgeon. His exact words will live with me forever: 'Oh shit, this has to come out.'

The 'wee tape' had eroded through my urethra like a cheese wire. He said it looked as though it had been in place for ten years, not ten weeks, such were the tissue adhesions to it.

I said I wanted the tape out immediately, but he told me it was very dangerous surgery and difficult to remove. I didn't care, I wanted it out.

I felt a strange kind of calm that night – at last I was believed, and I had hope that I'd soon be on the mend.

Next day, he took me back to theatre and when I came to after the operation I felt some immediate relief – my urethra was no longer being 'guillotined'. But that was not the end of my problems, not by a long way. My surgeon had only snipped and removed a small piece of the tape, as he said it was too dangerous to completely remove it. My left leg was giving way and when I tried to walk, the surgeon laughed and said I walked as if I was ice-skating… I didn't share his amusement. I later found out that this was due to obturator nerve damage. I was devastated to have gone through all that and still there was tape, which I later learned is polypropylene mesh, inside me.

Four weeks later, the pain was still hellish. It felt as though my groin, leg, buttocks and vagina were being tasered with electric shocks. I couldn't close my legs together because of some sort of obstacle that had a vice-like grip in my left groin. The urine infections were persistent, as were the painful pelvic spasms. I told the surgeon I could not live like this any longer. It was truly awful and my family were worried sick.

I was so badly infected they gave me more syringes of localised anaesthetic to take home to help numb the area, but they didn't even touch the pain, which was constant. I was in such a mess that the nurses couldn't manage to insert a catheter in me and they had to call a specialist midwife to try and help. It was the second-worst time of my life. I have to say I have never contemplated suicide, but if I had not had my kids then, perhaps Dignitas would have been an option. That is how bad it was.

Eventually, my surgeon agreed to remove all of the mesh. He said it was a very dangerous procedure as it was in a nerve-rich vascular area of the body. He said the bottom line is: 'You could die.'

I said, 'I feel like I am dying at the moment, so I have nothing to lose.'

He operated and told me that he had successfully removed all the mesh tape implant. I remained in hospital for five days, so that they could manage my pain with morphine and anti-sickness injections.

Although I'm better than I was, my life – our lives – have changed forever and not for the better. Our hopes and dreams are shattered. I have chronic pain due to nerve damage. I also have pelvic spasms and I am more incontinent than ever. I can manage a few steps with walking aids, but every step is painful. I need a wheelchair. My husband had no option but to take early retirement to look after me as I've fallen many times when my left leg has given way without warning. I have a stair lift, bath lift, bed rail, community alarm and copious amounts of medication just to manage on a daily basis.

All of this was the result of an elective surgical procedure – it was not life-saving surgery, it was completely avoidable. I had wrongly assumed that the 'wee tape' was similar to the contraceptive coil, something I thought I could try and if it didn't work it could be removed. When later I found it was a permanent mesh implant not intended to be removed I was flabbergasted – no one had told me this. If they had, I would never have agreed to it, no way!

OLIVE – No one told any of us it was permanent.

ELAINE – Prior to this operation, there was only medication. All I would take was two paracetamol if I had a bad headache, now I take over 20 tablets a day, some of them the strongest medicines you can take for nerve pain. I have developed high blood pressure, fibromyalgia, reactive inflammatory arthritis and diabetes. Also, I have low self-esteem at times.

In 2011, I came across and joined an email group based in England for women who had various types of transvaginal mesh implants. It was made up of around 50 women from England and one or two from Wales – I thought, naively, that I must be the only the person in Scotland affected. This group helped me no end. They understood.

Around this time my husband Jeff, a journalist with the *Paisley Daily Express*, was due to take part in the local 10k run. The paper ran a story highlighting that he was doing it to raise money for the charity 'TVT MUM' (Tension Free Vaginal Tape Messed Up Mesh), reporting how it had helped his wife after her mesh implant.

OLIVE – I saw the words 'TVT implant' in the story and as soon as I could I called into the paper's office and asked Jeff to get his wife to contact me. I also gave him some sponsorship money while I was there. Later that day, Elaine got in touch with me and I arranged to go and meet her at her house.

ELAINE – When Olive and I exchanged stories there were many similarities. In the coming weeks, we met another woman, Linda McLaughlin, from Greenock. Linda had had enough. She made her mind up to go public with her story. We said, 'Really?'

This was a brave decision, as no one really wants to talk about such personal intimate issues in public. By this time, we had carried out a lot of research and agreed to help with background information for the story.

We then received a call from a journalist at the *Sunday Mail*, Marion Scott, who wanted to cover Linda's story. As soon as it was published, another 50 women contacted the paper.

Marion came to us and said, 'What are we going to do with these women?'

Well, we didn't know what to do. We aren't medically trained, we were trying to cope with our own pain and medical conditions, but we felt we had to do something. Marion ran another story, then another, and each time she did, more and more women came forward until there were hundreds.

We started a group email and some of the women set up a Facebook page for Scottish Mesh Survivors so that no one would be on their own and they could chat to others who understood. We have hundreds and hundreds of women who have been injured or disabled by mesh in our group. It is indeed a scandal.

OLIVE – We think these numbers are just the tip of the iceberg as there will be many people who don't have the confidence or support to come forward; women who don't want to speak about this issue with anyone. I am really concerned for them and what they are going through. But with each article, more people come forward and now we have men coming forward who have had similar experiences with hernia mesh.

ELAINE – As far as we know, there are around 600 women taking legal action as a result of mesh in Scotland. There would be more but there is a three-year time bar on negligence cases and a ten-year bar on product liability. We know of some who have had mesh for up to 17 years before they experienced problems and completely unjustly they don't have any possibility of redress.

After Linda told her story, a group of us got together and decided we had to take this further, so we contacted the MSP Jackie Baillie who was the Shadow Health Secretary for Labour. A dozen of us met with her and Alex Neil, the Health Secretary. Alex listened and said they would set up a working group on the issue, which would include patient representatives.

Soon after this, Neil Findlay MSP replaced Jackie Baillie in the health role for Labour and he and his parliamentary researcher, Tommy Kane, met us immediately. After about ten minutes of discussion, Neil asked a straight question: 'Why the hell is the NHS still using this stuff? Why is it not banned?' For us it was a eureka moment – someone got it! Why indeed is mesh use not banned?

Following that meeting, there was a flurry of activity. Neil submitted dozens of written parliamentary questions. He asked questions of ministers, put in endless Freedom of Information requests and worked closely with us and Marion Scott to increase awareness, seek answers and build our knowledge base.

Whilst all of this was very helpful and worthwhile, it was hugely frustrating that mesh was still being implanted in Scottish patients. The clinicians and senior government officials and ministers stuck to the same line as the health regulators, the MHRA, that the benefits of mesh outweighed the risks because they'd received so few 'adverse event' reports from clinicians.

Then Neil and Tommy suggested we use the Parliament Petitions Committee to take things forward. This was the game-changer.

Jeff and I went to see our local MP, Jackson Carlaw, who listened intently and offered to do what he could to help us – he fully supported the petition route.

We worked on the petition's wording under Tommy's skilful direction. He helped us so much and we drew up six key points for the petition, lodged on 30 April 2014:

A Petition calling on the Scottish Parliament to urge the Scottish Government to:
1. Suspend use of polypropylene Transvaginal Mesh (TVM) procedures;
2. Initiate a Public Inquiry and/or comprehensive independent research to evaluate the safety of mesh devices using all evidence available, including that from across the world;
3. Introduce mandatory reporting of all adverse incidents by health professionals;
4. Set up a Scottish Transvaginal Mesh Implant Register with view to linking this up with national and international registers;
5. Introduce fully informed consent with uniformity throughout Scotland's health boards; and
6. Write to the MHRA and ask that they reclassify TVM devices to heightened alert status to reflect ongoing concerns worldwide.

The day the petition was heard was one of the most emotional days of our lives. I led off and took questions, Marion gave supporting evidence and Olive summed up at the end. One of the most dramatic moments was when Marion brought a piece of polypropylene mesh tape from her handbag and showed it to the committee, who were predominantly men. She showed them the sharp edges of the laser-cut plastic and asked them to imagine it moving inside a woman's pelvis as she walked and to envisage the damage it was doing to delicate tissue. It was graphic and powerful stuff, set against a backdrop of 70 sobbing mesh victims and their families.

OLIVE – The committee convener said it was the most powerful, emotional and highly charged meeting of the committee he had ever sat through.

After that meeting, Neil Findlay met Alex Neil and urged him to suspend mesh. He continued putting pressure on the government and Tommy helped us build up the evidence through extensive research.

ELAINE – Alex Neil was then called before the committee to answer the petition.

He used his appearance to 'request' that NHS boards suspend the use of mesh. Some acted and suspended its use immediately, but as we found out from subsequent FOI requests, Grampian, Lothian and Greater Glasgow health boards ignored the request and continued implanting hundreds of women. The government later claimed they couldn't direct surgeons to stop, they could only 'request' they stop implanting.

OLIVE – We didn't realise the clinicians could dismiss the Cabinet Secretary's 'request', but they did and around 800 women received an implant after the 'request' to stop.

ELAINE – It was only after the UK government moved to suspend mesh use in 2018 that we saw a full suspension here in Scotland. As all this was going on, Neil managed to secure time for a debate in parliament and we made sure we had a good presence of mesh-injured women and their families in the gallery for it. He called for a public inquiry into the issue, because it was now clear that mesh was becoming the biggest health scandal in the history of the Scottish NHS. With around 600 women submitting claims and goodness knows how many more sitting at home not having claimed, this was a major scandal.

The Scottish Government refused a public inquiry and instead announced an 'independent review'. We're told this is the tactic they use if they want a quicker and cheaper investigation into an issue – they are usually a very poor substitute.

However, Olive and I sat on the review as patient representatives and I recall us requesting a mandatory register of implants so that we could track what type of implant was being used, who implanted it, where the procedure was done, etc. This was so that if anything went wrong (just as would happen with a car with faulty brakes), the patient could be traced and there could be a recall. The Chief Medical Officer said of that, 'We are not North Korea yet! We cannot force clinicians to comply with a register, we have to dangle a carrot to encourage and incentivise them.' A remarkable quote. We also called for mandatory reporting of adverse incidents because at the time we launched our petition the NHS claimed there were only six complaints of adverse incidents in Scotland, yet 70 injured women sat in the petitions committee gallery alone, all having complained to their doctors about mesh – why were their cases not reported?

As the review proceeded, our demands and points were constantly rejected. Our comments were excluded from the review group minutes. They tried to sideline us and play down our view point at every opportunity. At one point, I asked one senior surgeon three times if she could perform full obturator mesh removal. After three non-answers, a senior member of review team reiterated the questions and said, 'Just answer the question – yes or no!' Of course, the answer came back that no, she couldn't. Afterwards, we were told there was a further discussion we weren't party to and a note was added to the minutes to say mesh 'could' be removed from the obturator in the first two to four weeks. This was changed to eight weeks and in the whitewash final report it was changed to 'may be possible anytime' by an experienced surgeon.

At one meeting, I was being cross-examined by three senior surgeons and officials who wouldn't let up and were pressing me aggressively on a number of issues. Now, I am not medically qualified, but I am knowledgeable about mesh and able to handle myself, so I answered everything, but they broke me under the intense pressure, so Olive stood up and wheeled me out and we left. We were not prepared to take that from them.

OLIVE – The reality is we had to fight for every word we wanted kept in those minutes and reports. They did everything to cut us out, dismiss our views and set aside our evidence.

ELAINE – We have participated in five different government groups in good faith and we regret participating in each and every one of them.

The original independent chair of the Review Group, Lesley Wilkie, proved to be an honest and fair person. She produced an interim report and while we did not agree with it all, it was all round a reasonably fair report. Then she resigned as chair and we never saw or heard from her again – it was claimed she resigned for 'personal reasons'.

A Scottish Government official stepped in (so much for the independence of the review) and said she wanted to publish the final report. At this point we had not been involved in any meetings for ten months but some of the others had. We found out that Sub group meetings had taken place without us knowing and we never saw sight of any minutes – we were excluded.

OLIVE – They then appointed a new chair who told us she was here to 'wrap this up quickly'. She was truly awful. Her manner was dreadful, arrogant and dismissive.

ELAINE – We were very concerned about the content of the review's final report and the way it was presented. We wanted it to be easily understood by the lay person, it wasn't, and they left out all negative references to mesh. They ignored our evidence and they buried Senior surgeon Dr Agur's supportive contributions, including patient friendly comparison tables that women could use to compare options and decide independently what was best for them. Dr Agur resigned from the review group in protest and it was clear to us that his opinion and supporting evidence had isolated him from the rest.

We were reaching the end of our tether but decide to appeal to the new Cabinet Secretary Shona Robison and the Chief Medical Officer, Catherine Calderwood for help but it was futile. They weren't prepared to delay publication of the final report to investigate our concerns of a whitewash review.

Reluctantly, we too decided to resign from the Review Group – it wasn't independent, it wasn't transparent – it had lost its way. There was no way we wanted our names associated with a whitewash report.

It was then Neil came up with the idea of getting a banner headed with a pledge calling for 'No mesh whitewash' and underneath we printed the names of every single MSP, with a space for them to sign.

We took about 25 mesh-injured women to Parliament and one Thursday, after First Minister's Questions, we pounced as MSPs were returning to their offices from the chamber, collaring over 100 MSPs from all parties to support the pledge – it was brilliant and really upped the ante. We didn't seek permission for this, we just did it and before the security officers realised what was happening they couldn't stop us. It was great, Neil and Tommy's plan worked a treat and we felt so proud of our women, who chatted with and educated MSPs, some of whom were keen to know more about how mesh affected us personally.

OLIVE – When the report came out there was an outcry it was a complete whitewash, it was one sided, ignored our views and painted a rosy picture of a product that was causing so much damage. Damage people could see in front of them when mesh-injured women spoke up. We called it a 'discredited sham' and produced a minority report, which gave our alternative view. Such was the outcry the government got Professor Alison Britton to conduct 'a review of reviews!' She slated the way it was conducted and came up with 43 recommendations about how to conduct any future independent reviews. Sadly, its recommendations have not been accepted in full.

ELAINE – What you have to remember is that when all of this was going on the women involved had to drag themselves out of their beds and wheelchairs, struggle many miles from across Scotland to get to Edinburgh, using their own money and were left knackered for days afterwards but they did it to try and push forward the campaign and to prevent others being injured by this potentially dangerous product – there was no personal gain for any of us.

Across the world, we are just one part of the global campaign but for our size, we have been very influential. We have had two US Attorneys work with us after noticing the Scottish campaign online and seeing Marion's fantastic articles. We have linked up with people in England, Wales and Ireland.

We know that in the US there are more than 100,000 mesh cases pending. We have worked with people in the US, Canada, New Zealand, Europe and Australia where it will be the biggest class action in their health care history. This is action against some of the biggest medical companies on earth, companies such as Johnson & Johnson and Boston Scientific.

OLIVE – Some of the pay-outs we see in the US are huge, but nothing will compensate for what women have lost. Some of the cases have used evidence from Scotland and referred to our petition during the case. At the bottom of all of this is corporate greed where companies sold a product they claimed was 'The Gold Standard treatment' but in reality, it is a damaging, horrible implant made from a material that was cheap, should never have gone into humans but ultimately was highly profitable for their shareholders.

ELAINE – Too many in the medical establishment still don't accept there is a problem with mesh. Some doctors and surgeons have been trained by the mesh companies and have bought into their propaganda and readily dismiss the concerns of patients. Some newer surgeons may not have been trained to perform traditional non-mesh repair surgeries and I believe health boards are worried that if mesh is banned they won't be able to treat patients. Dr Wael Agur is now offering training and retraining for surgeons using non-mesh surgical repair techniques. This is a more expensive option, which gets to the nub of the issue – cost. Profit for the mesh manufacturers is the key driver in all of this.

OLIVE – During the campaign we heard from the US Attorney Steve Mostyn, who had got his hands on internal documents from one of the companies who supplied the polypropylene. These documents showed that this polypropylene was not for use in humans. When the supplier stopped providing it to the mesh companies, the manufacturers used counterfeit product imported from a back-street supplier in China to ensure they continued to make money. The MHRA were alerted to this and said in a response that just because a product was counterfeit did not make it unfit for purpose. You couldn't make it up! They said as long as the device is performing it really didn't matter if it was counterfeit.

ELAINE – It is amazing – they will raid the Barras market in Glasgow for counterfeit DVDs or cigarettes yet allow potentially counterfeit plastic to be permanently implanted in humans. Steve Mostyn was representing thousands of US victims, he had unearthed so much information on the scandal but sadly and tragically he committed suicide – perhaps because of the pressures he was under. What a tragedy.

OLIVE – Our campaigning over the years has been driven by our desire to prevent others from experiencing what we have. We do not want any women to go through this hell. Previously there was no hope for us but recently there has been a glimmer.

ELAINE – We first came across Dr Dionysios Veronikis on US website Mesh Medical News Desk. He is a surgeon from St Louis, Missouri who has removed over 2,000 mesh implants using his innovative muscle and tissue sparing technique and his own specifically developed surgical instruments. We learned from him that mesh implants inserted via the groin required groin incisions to completely remove them – this makes sense.

OLIVE – And partial removal is often the worst option and can leave women even more debilitated than before. We've heard from women who have been told that the surgeons can't find their device or devices when they go into remove them. This is because being a permanent device and a mesh in structure, the body's tissue grows through it and embeds it in the body – it is not meant to come out. Trying to remove it is like trying to get chewing gum out of your hair and if not removed very carefully it can cause major internal damage to nerves and organs.

ELAINE – We have been trying to get the Scottish NHS to buy trans-labial ultrasound scanners (TLUS), which can show mesh clearly and is much cheaper option than a costly MRI which doesn't show mesh, only inflammation or mass. X-ray and CT imaging don't show mesh either but so far, our requests have been refused. Northern Ireland has a scanner, England has them but there are none here in Scotland. Women have to travel to England and pay upwards of £300 for a private scan. In addition to the financial cost, there is the added stress and impact a round trip of at least 800 miles has on their health.

Through discussions with Marion Scott, Dr Veronikis offered to come to Scotland to help women here and to train our surgeons by sharing his specialist skills and carefully honed mesh-removal technique – this gave many of us hope, especially those who have been written off by our surgeons. Frustratingly, the Scottish Government did nothing to progress his offer.

Neil Findlay then held a member's debate in the Scottish Parliament to raise Dr Veronikis' s offer and expressed deep frustration at the lack of any progress.

Many of us attended that debate to keep the pressure on Ministers to help us. Again, nothing happened, and Dr Veronikis became exasperated not just at the lack of progress but at the barriers being put in his way by senior clinicians in Scotland. He believed they were actively stopping him from coming here.

In the meantime, three Scottish women via the generosity of benefactors and crowdfunding raised the money to travel to the US for surgery. Dr Veronikis performed the mesh removal procedure. All of these patients said they had previously been told they had had full mesh removals in Scotland – yet all had up to 20cm of the stuff removed and photographed as evidence.

OLIVE – And the scandal of this is that when women in Scotland are complaining of problems, when they return again to their GP who has been informed by the hospital that their patient has had a full removal, they are not believed when they complain of pain and complications. The GP thinks they are making it up or it is all in their heads. This is not good for patients' mental health. Not being believed is one of the worst things about all of this. We have heard women saying they feel like walking in front of bus because of this.

ELAINE – The impact on people's lives is horrendous – we know women who have lost organs, lost their homes, their relationships, their jobs and incomes, their mobility, any quality of life they once had – women who have lost their lives. I personally haven't opened the blinds in my bedroom since 2011. My logic is that if I can't see out then people can't see in – I get upset when I speak about my own situation because it's still too raw.

OLIVE – For many their pain is not visible, but inside, their pelvic area is a car crash where they are experiencing excruciating pain and suffering, all the same symptoms as those who have more visible symptoms. For me there is far too much medical arrogance and big egos at play in all of this. I think they believed Elaine and I were 'two wee daft wifies' who they could brush aside at the meetings we attended and that we would not open our mouths. I felt like punching some of them with their arrogant, patronising, dismissive attitudes.

ELAINE – We have learned so much through this process, but the most important thing is to always ask questions. The days of seeing doctors or people in powerful positions as god have long gone. If you are to go through a medical procedure or treatment, ask about all the options and information available – you shouldn't need to but please do and do your research. Some will tell you not to look online – I have to say, the internet empowered me, it saved my life.

In relation to the campaign, Olive is the sister I never had, we work well together. But we couldn't have done this without the support of our husbands and family, they have encouraged us every step of the way. We have also built a close-knit network of people we trust with our lives – Marion Scott, Drs Wael and Karolina Agur, Tommy Kane, Neil Findlay (he got thrown out of Parliament for sticking up for us), MSPs Jackson Carlaw and Alex Neil – We call them Our 'Three Meshketeers', and lastly, my then MP Paul Masterton, who was the deputy chair of the Mesh All-Party Parliamentary Group at Westminster – he gave us a voice there. We have been through a huge amount together.

OLIVE – These experiences have shown me how powerful organisations like medical manufacturers and government manipulate situations to suit themselves not the needs of patients. How they fiddle the figures, use their legal officers to reinforce their position and discredit opponents or those with another view.

We have always tried to build cross-party support away from party politics and will always do so.

Our message to the campaigners of today is don't give up, be determined, speak out, build and use your networks, use your politicians, make demands of them, get the media on side, use the systems that are there, like the petitions committee, learn as you go and use that learning to advance your cause, that's our advice.

Scottish Mesh Survivors continue to campaign for all mesh victims to have the option of having their mesh removed by a surgeon of their choice, one who is fully versed in complete mesh removal. It is their view that no surgeon currently operating in Scotland meets this criteria.

PAUL QUIGLEY

The Football Act

Paul Quigley is a Lanarkshire boy from the 'new town' of Cumbernauld just outside Glasgow. From an early age, he was taken to football matches with his dad and uncles, following Glasgow Celtic. As a young supporter, he saw football as more than just a game; it was an expression of class, community, identity and collective values setting him and some of his fellow fans on a collision course with the increasingly corporate identity of the club and sport he loves.

In 2012 the Scottish Government introduced the Offensive Behaviour at Football Act in response to a high-profile, contentious and headline grabbing Celtic v Rangers football match where clashes on and off the field between players and management of both teams were beamed around the world. The act singled out football fans from the rest of the community subjecting them to a series of restrictive laws that curtailed civil liberties and free speech; it targeted young, largely working-class football supporters, leaving those who breached the act with a criminal record.

Unwilling to accept this attack on their rights, football fans fought back with a cross-club campaign, using innovative campaigning methods developed by involving and mobilising a network of grassroots activists. Paul Quigley became a key strategist and articulate advocate for the fans point of view. He and his fellow fans showed how effective organising, collectivism and passion combined with rational argument and political nous took on the establishment, overturned class prejudice, and won.

I HAVE SPENT all my life in Cumbernauld, one of Scotland's 'new towns'; it was completed in 1967. My parents came from the mining village of Moodiesburn. I have two younger brothers. My dad worked away quite a lot in the oil and gas industry, sometimes going offshore. Politics never dominated my growing up, but it was always on the fringes of the things. From when I was young, my dad and my uncle took me to football at Celtic Park. There was a big supporters' bus culture then, with groups organising coaches to home and away matches. Buses came from across the country. That type of supporter organisation is not as prevalent now; three buses ran from Moodiesburn in those days. My dad, uncle and one of their pals ran the three buses so I was immersed in it from an early age. But I think he didn't want me to just follow in their footsteps, so he took me to see the local team, Clyde FC, but from the moment I got there I was whingin and greetin to get home – it was freezing, the fitba was crap, the stadium rubbish, it was boring. You name it, they said I moaned about it. My dad realised Clyde weren't for me so from the age of about four or five I was going to see Celtic. I got my first season ticket in 1998.

For me football, politics and identity came together. We all get wisdom instilled in us from our parents and my dad drummed into me not to discriminate, to take people for who they are, to show respect. As I got older, I would steal and read some of his books on history or politics or world affairs. At the time, I was into American hip-hop music and this too helped politicise me. It was the time when the internet was becoming a universal, accessible thing, so I now had the power at my fingertips to find out information on any issue I was interested in. I started on the history of Scotland and Ireland (my family heritage is Irish). That led me to read about the Black Panthers, the political situation in Palestine and apartheid. I started to build my knowledge and understanding of the world and to understand class politics better. At the same time, I had a very inspiring Modern Studies teacher at my school, St Maurice's. When I was 16, I was hospitalised and had to have two operations. My teacher came to the hospital to tutor me. He was of a similar political persuasion, he was very influential. From around 16/17 I was politically engaged, not party political but I would have described myself as a socialist then and I'm a socialist now. Overall, I would say my political views developed from my family and community. It's there you learn values without really being aware of it, you are immersed in them and they become part of who you are. For me, I became motivated and wanted to have a positive impact on the community and world in which I lived.

Going through school wasn't plain sailing. I was a bit of a nightmare, I was a wee dick. There is no other way to describe my behaviour. I was typical of lots of young guys, education at that time wasn't the most important thing in my life. I was no different from many of my pals. The social aspect of school was more important to me than the academic side. I got into university by the skin of my teeth.

I had a bit of imposter syndrome at first, wondering how I got there. In first year, I spent too much time in the union, not the library, but I found that even doing the bare minimum I was doing better than most of my pals. In second year, my tutor Chick Collins pulled me in and gave me a verbal kick up the arse and told me I was underperforming and should be doing much better. It was exactly what I needed to hear. From then on, I got stuck in, my marks improved and I got a good degree in Sociology and Politics. I wanted to work for the trade union movement and so I went on to do a Master's in Human Resource Management in order to understand how the bosses thought and worked. I'm now in the first year of a PhD.

When I was about 16, I started going to football matches on my own but the football I was attending didn't reflect the stories I had heard from my dad and uncles. The atmosphere was flat, no one was singing, it was like a library, the football itself was turgid and uninspiring, you couldn't stand or be beside your mates (you couldn't stand at all, as it was all-seater stadiums with everyone dispersed across the ground). The supporters' bus culture was gone – the whole idea of a football and club community had disappeared. I don't go to football to watch 22 men kick a bag of wind about, that's not what excites me. I think a lot of young Celtic fans were probably rebelling against this new identity and supporters' groups with an overtly political identity sprang up. Young people in general in Scotland had been politicised by the anti-war movement around then (it was the aftermath of the Gulf War) and fans were opposing the appointment of former MP and Defence Secretary John Reid, now Baron Reid of Cardowan. It was this that motivated me to get involved in supporter politics.

It was a few years later that the Offensive Behaviour Act came about, all starting with the infamous 'game of shame'. During that season, Celtic had played Rangers seven times in league and cup matches – way too much, the teams and supporters were sick of each other. I went to every one of those games it had become boring, the atmosphere was gone, and the familiarity was breeding contempt amongst players, fans and coaching staff. That particular match in 2011 saw three Rangers players sent off, El-Hadji Diouf escorted off by the police, and Ally McCoist, Rangers assistant manager, and Celtic manager Neil Lennon getting into a fight on the touch line. By the time we got home from the match the media had gone apoplectic. Footage of the incidents was shown all across UK and international media channels. I got calls from friends in France and Italy asking if we were safe and if all was okay. The reality is that for us, for the fans, nothing happened: there were more Rangers players shown a yellow card that day than Celtic fans arrested. All of the issues were on the pitch, not off it. The majority of fan arrests were for the heinous crime of smoking in the toilets in the stadium. In terms of fan behaviour and conduct, there was no reason whatsoever for Scotland to go into the state of moral panic that it did. There was no violence, no evidence of arrests for hate crime or anything like that; the media had gone into hyper-sensationalism for what happened on the field of play.

In the aftermath, First Minister Alex Salmond convened an action group bringing together Celtic, Rangers, the Scottish Football Association, the Scottish Premier League, the police, the Church of Scotland, the Catholic Church, Nil by Mouth and others. It was around this time that Neil Lennon was sent bullets in the post and a 'viable bomb' was sent to another person. The narrative sped away from the reality of what had happened on the football pitch with the focus wrongly turning on the fans. At the same time, we were heading for the Scottish elections. The SNP government were determined to act and sought a flashy headline without any attempt to really understand what had gone on. Out of the action group meetings came the proposal for the Offensive Behaviour at Football Act.

After seeing the first draft of the proposed legislation, I met with a supportive lawyer in a pub in Glasgow and we ran through the bill line by line. By the time we had finished my head was mince. I knew we had to do something. This legislation was a catch-all that would allow the police scope to arrest anyone for doing anything that they found 'offensive'. That could mean almost anything. We realised we had to start organising to try and stop the act coming in. It would become a seven-year-long fight.

PROVISIONS OF THE BILL

The Offensive Behaviour at Football and Threatening Communication Act created two new offences – 'offensive behaviour at regulated football matches' and 'threatening communications'.

As well as applying to people actually attending matches, it also covered people travelling to and from matches, and those watching the match on TV in a pub.

It covered behaviour that was 'likely to incite public disorder' and which 'expressed hatred of' or 'stirred up hatred against' a person or group based on religion, race, nationality or sexual orientation.

The 'threatening communications' section of the law generally covered online and social media abuse.

The law was the first piece of legislation passed at Holyrood with no cross-party support, every SNP MSP voting in favour and every opposition MSP voting against.

The provisions of the law affected only football fans, no other sport.

We quickly contacted the five main Celtic fan organisations and a meeting was called with the Green Brigade, The Celtic Supporters' Association, the Celtic Trust, the Celtic Supporters' Affiliation and the Affiliation of Irish Celtic Supporters. These groups met and identified areas of the bill that specifically targeted fans of our club, but also the excessive and sweeping police powers that would have a big impact on fans across the country. We knew it was going to be difficult to disseminate our message and we put a lot of thought into how we would do that. Of the people who headed up these groups, among the few who had campaigning experience were Jeanette Findlay and former trade union official Joe Di Paola. Most of the rest had previously been in administrative roles in their respective supporters' groups. That was to change as they became campaigners.

Alex Salmond tried to bring the bill in as emergency legislation. In effect, he wanted to suspend democracy to address the fact that football players and managers had misbehaved, and young men were shouting and swearing at each other at a football match. It was absurd. Roseanna Cunningham MSP then went before the parliamentary justice committee to speak about the bill. Cunningham, a former advocate, put in a shocking performance saying at one point that she wanted to see people jailed for making 'an aggressive sign of the cross', whatever the hell that is. Even the Scottish media called out this nonsense. Salmond backed down from the emergency legislation route, changing tack to say that he now wanted to build consensus and the bill now would now go through the normal parliamentary process.

The Scottish elections took place in May 2011 with the SNP winning a majority. Buoyed by this, Salmond's version of consensus was to use very strong language to try and hammer the opposition parties into dropping concerns or opposition to the act, effectively saying that if you do not support this bill you are for sectarianism, which was of course utter nonsense. I have never met anyone who says they support bigotry or intolerance, but he used that language to pressurise MSPs. As the bill proceeded, the rhetoric intensified in an attempt to peel off opposition MSPs.

Our campaign stuck to a very clear message: first, you cannot outlaw something as subjective as 'offensiveness' without hindering freedom of expression; second, laws should be universal and you can't pick out one group of people (football fans) to apply such restrictive legislation.

In the first few months, we were fire-fighting, we didn't have a lot of time, we had to organise very quickly. We wanted to stop the bill, or at least dilute it. We stuck to our message, tried to build support amongst our own supporters, amongst pressure groups, other football fans and civil liberties organisations, and create a stir in the media. If we did this, then we hoped they would relent or at least water down their proposals.

But the truth is the SNP had a majority with no checks or balances and no interest in compromise – it was naive of us to think common sense might prevail in the end. The reality was, common sense didn't come into it.

To build support, we organised a demonstration at George Square in Glasgow. With thousands of people attending, this got a lot of media attention. We made big impact statements at matches, unfurling banners with satirical imagery at each game. We contacted fan groups at Rangers, Motherwell, Hamilton, etc. We knew it wouldn't be beneficial for our activists to, say, go to Hamilton or Motherwell to speak about the act and try to convince them of our case, that just wasn't going to happen, so we had to trust others to organise their people as they best understood that support and that community. There were good communications between groups and key individuals from their fan groups and each updated their supporters about the latest developments. Each group had its key activists providing leadership. We understood that this was the best way of galvanising supporters in individual clubs.

As the bill made its way through Parliament, we ran a mass email campaign hosted through the Celtic Trust website, with thousands of emails going to MSPs. We lobbied the Justice Committee members who would be taking evidence. Our focus had moved to changing public perception and influencing the debate in Parliament. Many of us had some political knowledge, but we had never campaigned or organised campaigns like this before. We were learning but also making it up as we went along.

It was clear to us that class was the underpinning element of the bill. A citizen could attend a rugby match or the horse racing or any other sporting event and behave in a certain way, and there would be no impact; but if you behaved in the same way at a football match, you faced fines, imprisonment and a criminal record. This was a clear attack primarily on young working-class men and women.

As the football season progressed, so did the bill and discussions about it. It took us time to build links to sympathetic parliamentarians. We got help from MSPs Michael McMahon and Hugh Henry, who asked questions in Parliament, spoke at events and gave support, but the bill was passed with the SNP using its majority to vote en-bloc to support it. All of the opposition parties opposed it.

After the act came into effect, the atmosphere on the terraces changed. Fans could feel the attitude of the police hardening. There was a shift in the culture of policing, it was palpably more aggressive and intolerant. And with that, they did our job for us. Fans were being arrested and charged under circumstances we hadn't seen before, and everyone attending matches could see the injustice of it. People who had been football fans for 40 or 50 years with no history of any trouble saw their supporters' buses stopped and searched and they were filmed. The relationship between the police and fans became poisoned. At an away European match in France, a Scottish police officer who I didn't know and had never met before came up to me and said, 'All right, Paul, how are you getting on at uni?' That was clearly intended to intimidate me. It was the type of thing you see in the movies when they are dealing with organised crime!

The surveillance was really in your face. From the moment we stepped off a supporters' bus or a flight we were followed and filmed until the moment we got back on.

More and more people were being arrested for things they would never previously have been arrested for and they were being treated far more harshly by the justice system. It was incredibly vindictive. Some were arrested for singing songs about people who were covered by protected characteristics like race or gender or ability and I have no problem with that, but because the police had greater scope, they went after people singing songs with historical, political or cultural references. People were being arrested for swearing at opposition fans or at the ref. One person I knew saw his friend being stopped outside the stadium by the police and when he approached the officer to ask if there was 'a problem', the officer turned around and said, 'Did you just call me a fucking prick?' He then grabbed the guy, marched him back into the ground and arrested him there so that it was an offence under the act, meaning he would receive a football banning order.

Such incidents were reported to us every week from fans. Sadly, the big clubs like Celtic were complicit in this approach; it took them a long time to properly begin to defend supporters who had been targeted. This led to tension within our five supporters' groups. Some were not as comfortable at challenging the club as others, but as the arrests ratcheted up, pressure intensified.

A number of us basically did crash-courses to establish what advice we could give fans caught up in all of this. People were having to attend every court in person and we would put them in touch with lawyers. If the case was being heard a long way from the accused's home, then that could jeopardise their employment. There was no plea bargaining on any cases under the act – every charge was prosecuted, and the accused were banned from attending football matches. Cases went on far longer than normal court cases and people lost their jobs because of taking time off. Some suffered from mental ill health or relationship breakdown, had their names dragged through the media and were alienated from their social circles. Even if they were eventually found not guilty, by that time the damage had been done. The human cost was collateral damage in the propaganda war led by the government. All of this went on for a year before events at the Gallowgate in the East End of Glasgow in March 2013.

On that day, a small march was planned in solidarity with banned supporters, with Celtic fans heading up the Gallowgate towards the stadium. There had also been another event planned in Glasgow that day by the racists of the Scottish Defence League, but it had passed without any real issue, as only three fascists and a dog had turned up. Later, Chief Constable Stephen House claimed the SDL event was the reason for 400 police, a helicopter, 40 horses and 20 riot vans being on duty in the East End, where fans were due to walk to the match, as thousands did every other week. The crowd set off to avoid the police and walk to the ground; as we started to make our way, it all kicked off. The police waded in and arrested people, held people down with their feet on their back, kettled us for long periods, filmed us, attacked us, drew their batons and really just tried to send a message to fans. One officer remarked that the police approach during this time was one of 'shock and awe', and this day characterised that better than any. It was appalling. It was something I have never seen before or since, it was brutal.

A few days later the chief constable wrote to every MSP claiming that fans were drunk, violent thugs who were out of control and that Police Scotland footage would be released to show this once they were convicted. A few MSPs raised concerns about the attacks on us and they were condemned for doing so. The cases came and went and only two convictions were secured, one for someone being in possession of illegal drugs (nothing to do with the event) the other for resisting arrest after the police had waded in on the fans. Everyone else who was arrested was found not guilty. The video footage was never released.

Week in, week out, the legislation became less and less credible. It was universally despised by football supporters. If you can get Celtic and Rangers fans to agree on anything, that is an achievement – and they did on this. It would have been easier to get UKIP and the Green Party to agree (mind you, even they agreed on this terrible act!). The bill only found allies in the Holyrood bubble of the governing party, who had no idea about football or how it worked. With the independence referendum in full flow in 2014, everything else took a back seat, including the Fans Against Criminalisation campaign, but arrests still came.

Post referendum, we decided to reinvigorate the campaign with the launch of a petition in 2015. It was not at that time about getting it to the Petitions Committee in Parliament – at that point it was to allow us to get out and speak to people and have conversations about the issues at stake. Our petition really took off and we quickly got 20,000 signatures. Then we realised we could now take it to Parliament, right into the seat of power and challenge the act directly. By this time, the architect of the legislation, Justice Secretary Kenny MacAskill, had been sacked by Nicola Sturgeon and was now a member of the Petitions

Committee. We thought this would be a bit of an opportunity.

When the legislation was originally passed, there was a clause saying that there should be a review within a set period. The SNP tried to claim that a very limited piece of research by academics at Stirling University could constitute the review, despite the academics themselves stating clearly that it wasn't. They then released a YouGov poll to try and justify not having a review. It was ludicrous, childish nonsense. The questions asked were embarrassing. We expected a similar process to the original committee sessions, where everyone with an interest, including the football community, would have its say, but we were to be denied this in a blatant ploy to avoid scrutiny. So we made our petition about the question of the review and in January 2016, me and Jeanette Findlay went to Parliament to appear before the Petitions Committee.

At the time, I was working part-time in a call centre while doing my Master's and an internship as part of it. I had very little time to prepare for the hearing. On the train through, I had to do interviews on Radio Scotland and some other media, it was all a bit rushed and frantic. I never ever thought I would find myself in this situation, it had kind of been thrust upon me. The only comforting presence on the committee was Michael McMahon, the MSP who had given us most support, who at that time convened the committee. Some of the others were openly hostile or at best ambivalent.

I gave a concise opening statement and then the chair opened up the discussion for questions. I have to say, this committee session changed the campaign. Macaskill, who is lawyer by profession, was clearly raging that we had the gall to be there and he came over very, very hostile. He was like an angry drunk slumped at the bar, fuming that he had to even acknowledge us. His body language was saying, who the fuck do these people think they are? He went on full attack and it was clear he wanted us to go down to the level he was operating at, but we refused to do that. We didn't rise to his provocation. He clearly thought me, a daft wee football supporter, was beneath him. He spoke to me very differently from how he spoke to my colleague Jeanette Findlay, no doubt because I'm much younger. He came across as a bully, losing the plot really.

In the coverage that followed, people reacted to this former justice minister in all-out attack on me, a wee guy from Cumbernauld who cares about football and football fans. It didn't look good for him on TV afterwards. After the session, I went to work. My phone had packed in, so I could not assess how it had gone. By the time I got home it had all gone crazy. I was getting supportive and congratulatory messages from across the country, fan forums were going wild, the media was covering it.

From that day, we gained huge credibility. We proved we could take our case out of the football arena and into the political arena and successfully and professionally present our case. We took on the minister responsible for bringing in the hated legislation and by most people's reckoning we came out on top, staying calm and focused all the way through.

The whole parliamentary episode increased our confidence, raised our morale and gave us real credibility. Previously, journalists hadn't really engaged with us – investigative journalism in Scotland is in a grim state – but now journalists took us seriously, came to us for comment and followed up on our stories.

Throughout the committee session, James Kelly MSP sat in on the discussion and afterwards he said that if he was re-elected at the forthcoming election he would bring in a member's bill to repeal the act. We thought well this a bit fanciful, as the SNP looked like they were going to secure another majority and it was highly unlikely Kelly would retain his seat. I wasn't convinced he would be there to introduce the repeal bill, but I was thrilled to be proved wrong.

We tried to get Nicola Sturgeon to comment on the act but in seven years she refused to do so, not a single word did she utter.

At the 2016 election, the SNP narrowly lost its majority. James Kelly was returned as a List MSP for Glasgow. There was a glimmer of hope for us. If we could keep the coalition of disparate opposition parties together and prevent the SNP picking off a few individual MSPs, we had a chance. The stars aligned a bit – it was pure luck.

During that summer parliamentary recess, we worked with James and others to draft the bill to repeal the act. For the next two years we kept the campaign going. We worked behind the scenes to brief each of the parties and keep them on board and ensure supporters remained focused.

The Offensive Behaviour at Football Act made history as the first ever bill to introduced by the Scottish Parliament to subsequently be repealed. We had won, seven years of campaigning paid off. The moment of the vote being read out was quite incredible for a group of ordinary people who had taken on the might of the Scottish Government and somehow managed to come out on top. Relief flooded through my veins. Leading the campaign for as long as Jeanette and I did, we knew just how many people were relying on us getting it over the line. Many people had suffered as a result of the act, others were coming up on petty charges and many feared they might be next if it wasn't repealed. The responsibility weighed heavy on me and to know in that moment there was a victory for all these people was an incredible feeling.

When I look back on what we achieved, I can't help but be in awe of the depth of passion and resilience in my community, and of the depth of skill and innovation that we could tap into amongst our supporters. Every time a great idea came forward, or a suggestion was made, we were able to execute it because of the people we could call on. If we wanted an email campaign that would maximise the impact of what we were doing, we could call on computer coders to do that. If we wanted high impact advertising of an event, then we had graphic designers who would help. When we made podcasts or videos, we could call on sound and video engineers or producers. Not once did we go to a company or professional body or have to pay for these things. We had a small core group organising, but a wealth of talent and commitment we could call on at any time.

The political element of all of this was, in my view, a tactical consideration by the SNP government that there were votes to be had for them in this act, and that in the opposition, they were dealing with a group of daft working-class bams, bigots and alcoholics who wouldn't have the wherewithal, knowledge or resources to fight back. If that was how they saw us it was a major miscalculation. They didn't realise the depth of feeling, passion and ability among football fans galvanised by the sense that we were being victimised. For myself and others at the forefront of the campaign, we were backed the whole way. This was what contributed to our victory most. Some SNP MSPs apparently believed we were being funded by some sort of 'dark money'. What that attitude really implied was: there is no way these people can be this effective on their own, some sinister forces must be helping them behind the scenes. This was actually a compliment to our collective effort. I am so proud of the campaign, the Celtic support, Scottish football fans and the working-class people who stood up against an attack on their rights. We never shirked from the scale of the challenge. We challenged a majority government, took on a complicit national police force, challenged those who should have spoken out in Parliament and we succeeded.

Ultimately, it was ill-advised to pick a fight with us, because we had nowhere else to go. We had no one else to rely on, so we faced the battle head on. It was up to us as football fans to challenge this draconian legislation and we did. It's the same with the Living Wage or the Living Rent campaigns, the people best placed to fight back and lead are those who are affected by these issues. If some injustice affects your community and who you are, then you have to take action, don't wait on someone else.

Our resilience was built on knowing we were fighting for our rights. We knew that the people we cared about will always outlast politicians or bureaucratic pen-pushers making laws. If you organise and mobilise and draw on the vast well of talent that is there in working-class communities, you can indeed change things for the better.

LOUISE ADAMSON

Michael's Story

Louise Adamson is a quiet, dignified woman who was thrust into activism and campaigning when her brother Michael, a young electrician, was electrocuted and killed at work. Louise and her family refused to accept the company line that blamed his workmates for Michael's death and instead sought to pursue truth and justice through the courts.

Following a painful, extended delay, they were failed by the justice system. Unwilling to sit back and watch as similar tragedies were inflicted upon other families, Louise decided to channel her grief into positive action and started to share Michael's story with workers, trade unionists, companies and communities – anyone who would listen.

She campaigned to change the law on corporate homicide, working with politicians in an attempt bring in legislation that would hold companies responsible for failings that resulted in the loss of life of their employees.

Louise now works internationally educating people about the true cost of poor health and safety at work. She also supports workers, communities and families through the Scottish Hazards Centre.

I GREW UP in Granton, Edinburgh. I went to the local Holy Cross Primary School and St Augustine RC Secondary. My dad was an engineer who started out in the merchant navy, but once marriage and we kids came along, that put paid to his sailing days. He then worked in various engineering roles in a number of businesses based in Leith Docks, Edinburgh more widely and Fife, until he retired aged 65. Through the '80s and '90s he was made redundant a few times, like many other industrial workers at that time. We weren't unusual in having a bit of that to contend with, growing up.

My mum worked for the Bank of Scotland when she first left school. Again, when we came along, things changed and she stopped working to look after us. She went back to work when we were settled at school, first as a domestic in the Victoria Hospital and then returning to the Bank of Scotland, latterly in Human Resources, until she took voluntary severance when Bank of Scotland and Halifax merged.

Growing up, I was football daft – both playing and watching. I followed Celtic, not the Edinburgh teams, Hearts – who my brother supported – or Hibs – my dad's team. I saw the light, that's what I like to say!

At school I'll admit to having been a bit of a swot, who bumbled along. Initially I wanted to be a PE teacher, but teachers convinced me I should be following a different career route and I ended up applying for university to study Law.

The choice of university was between Aberdeen and Edinburgh. Among other factors, Aberdeen would have been a stretch on the money front, so I stayed at home and went to Edinburgh with a view to becoming a lawyer. During my time at university, I did a summer work placement at a law firm as part the admin team, doing various tasks for the lawyers. Seeing up close how some of them acted, I came to thinking that there was no way I want to end up like that – superior, talking down to people, full of their own self-importance. It wasn't me. I had no intention of going down that route.

So, when I left university with my Honours degree, I had no job to go to. I was looking for HR jobs and also applied for a place in the TUC organising academy – I really didn't know what I wanted to do, I just knew it had to be centred on ensuring the world of work was a fairer place.

I loved Employment Law and Labour Law when I was at university. It was the subject taught by my Director of Studies, Dr Douglas Brodie, and there was a great focus on collective bargaining and industrial conflict. It sparked something in me and was the only subject I got a first for.

Dr Brodie (now a professor) put me in touch with a niche employment law firm as he thought that I would fit in really well and following an interview with the two named partners, I started work with Mackay Simon as a Research

Assistant. I was initially taken on to work 16 hours a month, but within a couple of weeks, they asked me to go full-time. During that period, I came to see that not all lawyers are like those I'd encountered during my summer placement – very far from it! – and so I took the decision to go back to university to complete my Diploma in Legal Practice and ended up doing my traineeship, qualifying with them.

We did work for both employer and employee clients, and a couple of teaching trade unions. I worked for them for 13 years, though I only did the frontline casework for maybe six or nine months. A sex discrimination case against a major hotel chain over maternity leave was the only time I was in a full employment tribunal providing representation. And, to use a footballing analogy: played one, won one, retired undefeated. That was because I then moved into a professional support lawyer role, which involved undertaking research for others, writing articles and client updates putting together training materials, delivering training, that sort of thing.

All in all, life was going along quite nicely.

Then in 2005, my brother was killed at work.

Michael was an electrician with Mitie Engineering Services (Edinburgh) Limited. He was 26 years old and engaged to be married. He was a big bundle of fun, the one who brought the patter and banter wherever he went. The one who thought of others ahead of himself and who would light up any room he entered.

He left the house on the morning of 4 August 2005 and didn't make it home. His employer was a subcontractor on a construction contract to build a JJB sport store and gym complex in Dundee. It was coming to the end of the job and it was an all hands on deck job to get it ready. It needed to be handed over to the client at ten o'clock the next morning, or else their penalty clauses were going to kick in. Michael didn't start the day on that job. He started the day at a job in Fettes in Edinburgh but got called up to Dundee in the afternoon.

I remember that day, I had been at work and then I'd gone off to do a bit of late-night shopping before I headed home. I was making my dinner a wee bit later when the phone rang, and it was my mum. She said Michael had been in an accident in Dundee and she and my dad were in the car heading over the Forth Road Bridge to get to Ninewells Hospital. They didn't say what sort of accident, or what condition he was in. I just knew we had to get there. I jumped in the car with my husband and we set off. There were some phone calls on the drive up and I just knew from the nature of the conversation that I was hearing that this was not good.

When I got out at Ninewells hospital I could see my mum and dad standing up at the door of Accident and Emergency and I just knew Michael was dead.

I knew because, had he been alive they would have been at his bedside. I collapsed at the side of the car as I got out. I just knew from the look of them that he was gone.

When we went into the hospital, Michael's fiancée was there along with their two best pals, Ian and Alison. I cannot explain the horror, it felt like an out of body experience. We were escorted into this dark, grey room and there he was, lying, horrifically, 'at peace'. A son, brother, fiancé and best friend, who had been the life and soul, whose life had been taken from him.

Management from Mitie were at the hospital too, as were the police. And while I don't remember fully what was said that night, a police officer said they would be in touch and would get us details of what was needed and would find out when Michael's body would be returned to Edinburgh... all the 'formalities'.

I vividly recall the drive to Dundee. I remember what songs were on the radio. I remember turning off The Hollies, 'He Ain't Heavy, He's My Brother', and firing in a mixed tape, only to hear Johnny Bristol singing 'Hang On In There'. I remember all that and I remember the calls – I don't know how I drove back down the road.

My mum and dad had been worried they were going to run out of fuel on the way to the hospital and so they had to stop at the garage just outside Dundee on the way back.

When we all got back to Edinburgh, we sat up all night at mum and dad's – no sleep, trying to come to terms with the horror of what had happened. My mum and dad had to phone people to tell them the news, in shock. From there, in the days afterwards it was a constant stream of people coming into the house, just disbelieving.

The funeral was a week the following Friday at St Margaret Mary's Church in Granton. He died on the 4th but we had to wait until the 12th for the funeral to take place. It was the same day as the MP Robin Cook's funeral was being held at the city's St Giles Cathedral. St Margaret Mary's church is less than a five-minute walk along the road from my mum and dad's house. The undertaker walked along in front of the hearse. It was a road we'd scarpered along to mass together as children, so this was utterly surreal. After the church, we went to Warriston Crematorium and got stuck in traffic on the narrow roads that lead to it. Bizarre as it seems, we joked in the car, saying it was meant to be Robin Cook who was bringing the city to a standstill today, not Michael Adamson.

The reality is we shouldn't have been laying to rest my 26-year-old brother.

Thinking back to the time between Michael dying and the funeral, we had to deal with the arrangements and felt let down by agencies like the police. We were told on the night of his death that they would be in touch the next day to tell us when his body was being returned, but we heard nothing – and ultimately ended up with the Chief Inspector of Tayside Constabulary in my mum and dad's front room apologising for the way they had treated us.

Bereaved families should be treated better than this and we demanded a Family Liaison Officer. Why should we not have one? We were the victims of a crime and why should we not have police support. The one that we did get was amazing.

Then... I suppose it is kind of fortunate for my family that I had the background as a lawyer, so I knew that we needed representation. I already knew about Thompsons Solicitors, and the work that Patrick McGuire and the team did. My pal Toni worked for them; we got in touch and Syd Smith took on the case.

The HSE report showed that there were management failures and that basic controls on site were absent.

The case then went to the procurator fiscal to consider whether or not there should be a prosecution. We had a hell of a time with the procurator fiscal's office. We would get told we'd receive an update in a week's time or in a month's time, but we were always left chasing for that update.

I went back to work just a fortnight after Michael's death because I couldn't bear the emptiness and helplessness of the days, I needed to have my mind occupied by something else. My dad also returned to work some months afterwards. But my mum had taken the voluntary severance from the bank. She had intended to go back to work in due course, but after what happened, she felt she couldn't – she couldn't face having to explain to new colleagues what had happened to us. This meant she was often the one who was left chasing answers, phoning the fiscal's office repeatedly. We went through seven or eight different procurator fiscals over a three-year period before we eventually got to trial. And three years is quick, a family will often have to wait upwards of five years until a health and safety case like this gets to court!

When the circumstances of Michael's death did eventually come to trial, Mitie Engineering Services (Edinburgh) Limited were charged. So too were managing director Billy Mitchell, the operations director Scott Wallace and the technical services manager Ian Storrar, all charged with criminal health and safety offences. No case to answer submissions were submitted on behalf of the three individuals once the Crown's case was finished. Sadly, those were accepted and they were released from the dock. This was, in my opinion, down to mistakes by the prosecutor and evidence not being led from the correct witnesses.

In the end, the three individuals got off scot-free. The look that I got from the managing director as he was released from the dock said, 'Why the fuck have I been sitting in there for the last four weeks?' There was no attempt to take responsibility for what had happened. Summing up, the advocate for Mitie said his client, 'the company', was now the invisible man sitting in the dock. It was that 'invisible man' who was found guilty and fined £300,000.

I was disgusted, and we maybe would have believed this level of injustice was a one-off, were it not for the fact that about a year after Michael's death I found out about FACK, Families Against Corporate Killing, a new campaigning and support organisation for those whose loved ones had been killed by work.

It was through my work as an employment lawyer that I found out about them, doing some research for a client update, a TUC Risks Bulletin arrived in my inbox and it announced FACK's launch.

Hilda Palmer from the Greater Manchester Hazards Centre, along with a number of other families she had been supporting, were the core group of families involved. They are now lovely enough to count me as one of their founding members, even though I wasn't in with the bricks. I was, however, the first person to approach them for support after they had set up and launched the group. If I'm honest, I didn't really know what I was in touch with them for at first. I very tentatively fired off an email and told them what had happened to us. And I was invited down for a meeting with the other founder FACKers:

Dawn and Paul Adams – son, Samuel Adams, aged six,
killed at Trafford Centre, 10 October 1998.
Linzi Herbertson – husband, Andrew Herbertson, 29,
killed at work in January 1998.
Mike and Lynne Hutin – son, Andrew Hutin, 20,
killed at work on 8 Nov 2001.
Mick & Bet Murphy – son, Lewis Murphy, 18,
killed at work on 21 February 2004.
Linda Whelan – son, Craig Whelan, 23, (and Paul Wakefield)
killed at work on 23 May 2004.
Dorothy and Douglas Wright – son, Mark Wright, 37,
killed at work on 13 April 2005.

On the way down on the train, I was reading a book entitled *How to Win Campaigns*, intent on being full of great new ideas when I arrived in Manchester. I didn't have a clue about the power of work Hilda Palmer had done over many decades and will admit to feeling a bit of a tool on discovering that what she didn't know about campaigning wasn't worth knowing. Decades of working in the trade union and Hazards movement will do that for you! I thankfully learned to listen fast and to draw on the vast knowledge and experience.

There is no way I'd have the strength to be doing what I'm doing now had I not found Hilda and my fellow FACKers. I will be forever in their debt, because finding them has ensured that positives have come from the awfulness of Michael's death.

FACK was initially set up to lobby against the Corporate Manslaughter and Corporate Homicide Act, which is as weak and toothless as we said it would be. There has been not a single successful prosecution in Scotland under this legislation. We said it was not going to get the big businesses that it needed to, it was only going to get small businesses (which were already being caught by the law) – and so it has proven.

The CMCHA has a 'senior management' test, rather than a 'management failure' one, which we argued would enable larger organisations with complex devolved management systems to stay 'off the hook'. There was no provision for the prosecution of individual directors or senior managers who would take decisions, or fail to take action, which then resulted in the death of a worker or member of the public. And the punishment for committing the offence of corporate manslaughter or corporate homicide was to remain a fine… a punishment which does not fit the crime.

We wrote to and lobbied MSPs and MPs, we talked to trade unions and pressure groups, we spoke at the Scottish Parliament and Westminster, we presented at the Centre for Corporate Accountability and held demonstrations. Though we were ultimately unsuccessful in getting the legislation changed before it ended up on the statute book, we have not relented in, as Hilda puts it, 'speaking truth to power'. It was through my contact with FACK that I was also put in touch with the Scottish Hazards Campaign and met Ian Tasker who was assistant secretary responsible for health and safety at the STUC at the time. As a result, I was asked to speak at a Scottish Labour Party Conference in Oban. This was around 18 months after Michael's death. At the time, Karen Gillon MSP was putting forward her alternative proposals to change the law on corporate homicide.

The experience was absolutely brutal, not just for me but for everybody in the room who had to watch me suffering, trying to speak. But it helped. A lot. And what I've found since is that I've found my voice.

At school I wouldn't have spoken in front of my class. In English, I used to have to get taken off to a side room with a few of my classmates to do any speaking tasks. Same through university. The fear of public speaking was full-on. But at Michael's funeral, his pal Ian had spoken and then I did too. Initially, there was no way on God's earth that I was going to do it. It was Michael's fiancée, Leasa's mum – a teacher – who said: 'If you don't do it, you're going to regret it.'

Speaking in front of hundreds of people at your wee brother's funeral was quite a way to be cured of that initial fear of public speaking, but to then be able to channel that into campaigning for change has been invaluable to my process of healing following Michael's death. Telling the human story behind the need for a change in health and safety practices, procedures or attitudes is the most effective way to make positive change happen.

I've also been able to channel my energies in other ways to prevent future loss of life or of a loved one.

The Scottish Hazards Campaign had been in existence since long before I got involved. They had always wanted to have an advice centre for workers, but had never ever had the money to make that ambition a reality. But we kept up the pressure and in 2014/15 we got some seed money to establish it. We figured, if we don't do this now, we never will, so with just £20,000 or so we moved to launch the Scottish Hazards Centre.

This came about at a point when I had just started telling 'Michael's Story' to businesses and organisations. I was asked by the steering committee for Scottish Hazards, which included Ian Tasker, Kathy Jenkins, Scott Donohoe and John Docherty, if I could take on the project to set Scottish Hazards on a charitable footing ahead of launching the advice centre. I was a bit nervous about it, as we wanted to have another child and I had a stable and long-held job at the law firm, with maternity leave and decent conditions. But I said to myself, 'Do you know what? You're never going to be asked to do this again, this is a one-off thing that needs done.' It was a leap of faith, one I'm so grateful I had the opportunity to take.

The Scottish Hazards Centre launched in October 2015, providing advice, support and training to workers on all aspects of occupational health and safety. We are supported by Thompsons Solicitors, who host a phone line for us (0800 0015 022) fielding calls and passing to our advisers to take forward. Our lead adviser is Ian Tasker, who not only undertakes advice and representative work, but also continues to work on policy development and heads up the work needed for International Workers' Memorial Day across Scotland.

The Centre has dealt with all manner of issues, including: asbestos, temperature in work places, disciplinary action after having raised health and safety issues, and more recently, COVID-19. We've also had managers in touch who have been targeted for trying to do the right thing. And we have provided support to community action groups, for example the parents of pupils at Buchanan and St Ambrose High Schools. This is all aimed at preventing death, injury and illness. Ian is also providing support to families seeking justice for lost loved ones, seeking to ensure in the process that lessons are learned and nothing similar ever happens again. It is hugely important and hugely rewarding work.

For me, my 'day job' is that of 'workplace safety speaker'. I go to organisations and talk through the failings that led to Michael's death and the impact that has had on family, friends and colleagues, making health and safety a much more real thing. I obviously wish I wasn't doing it, but I am grateful to have found the strength to do so. It does help me, as I see the positive impact talking about what happened to Michael has on people. You see the changes that happen in workplaces, witness the changes in attitudes. You hear people walk in grumbling, 'Jeez, another health and safety presentation… wait until you hear the hot air in here!' Then you see those same people walk back out going 'I get it.'

I speak to all sorts of different firms: marine, construction and utilities companies, food businesses and the pharmaceuticals industry in the UK and further afield, in Sweden, Denmark, Holland, Germany and Australia.

Progress is made by collective effort. That is how you bring about change. I wouldn't be doing any of what I'm doing now had I not found FACK. Absolutely no way. Knowing that I wasn't howling solo into the wind is what helped me to find my voice and realise that I can be a voice for others. This brings a huge amount of comfort to me. In campaigns, you need good people around you who understand the positives of what you're aiming to achieve. For me, it was important they didn't just see the misery and devastation of what happened, but that we were trying to turn that into positive good. It's not about wallowing, it's not about self-pity: it's about making positive change for other people.

A word of caution. People must know they are not necessarily going to change the world overnight. Don't have unrealistic expectations. When I set out I was quite naive; I thought we were going to get Karen Gillon's Corporate Homicide Bill through in the Scottish Parliament. Yet here we are – bloody hell, how many years later – backing Claire Baker as she brings forward the latest incarnation of these proposals, still trying to right the wrongs foisted on families who lose loved ones in work-related incidents. I've often been far too naive and thought that we could bring about change like that [finger snap]. But don't let the pace of things get you down or dampen your drive, because you know what? Know that you are right! You need to keep at it, keep speaking the truth, and eventually you are going to turn enough people the right way… your way!

Epilogue

IT WOULD BE easy to despair at the state of the world today. But we must not. Indeed, we cannot.

Gaza is in flames; the climate crisis shows no sign of abating; and school and community shootings continue across the US. In England, the Tories have won the local elections. Meanwhile, Labour leader Keir Starmer slumps from tedium to disaster. In my homeland, the conversations in the run-up to the elections to the Scottish Parliament were dominated by constitutional wrangling. Even so, I take heart from the stories of the ordinary people featured in this book who stepped up to become genuine heroes. They are not the only ones. A few recent campaigns immediately spring to mind.

Just recently in Glasgow, Home Office vans turned up to deport two asylum seekers. They were stopped from doing so by a huge demonstration of solidarity from the local community. This spontaneous direct action was an inspiring response from decent people concerned for their fellow human beings.

In the midst of the Covid crisis, the Scottish and UK governments attempted to impose an exams system that used an algorithm which discriminated against working-class pupils, basing results not on individual performance but on the past record of individual schools. Thousands were disadvantaged. What followed was an organic uprising of anger and action and in the space of a week there was a policy U-turn. Pupil power won.

In the hospitality, food and service sectors, workers sick of being patronised and applauded as 'key workers', but paid a pittance while on precarious contracts, are fighting back and organising on many fronts to take on the big corporations.

As long as there is injustice, there is the opportunity to join – or even start – a campaign to set things right.

You might decide to join the response to the drugs deaths crisis in Scotland that sees 1,200 of our fellow citizens die unnecessarily every year.

You might want to join those who are taking on the big pharma companies who created the opioid crisis through their marketing of addictive painkillers and antidepressants, or those who are taking the government and medical establishment to task over the lack of mental health services in our communities.

You might add your own voice to the demand for government action to end poverty, inequality, homelessness and landlordism.

You might opt to seek justice for the families of elderly care home residents who died as a result of so-called 'mistakes' in discharge policy over the last 18 months.

As causes and crises develop, new champions will emerge – ordinary people who are galvanised into action by a desire for decency and fairness.

People who will challenge and fight the powerful.

People who will campaign for, and deliver, justice.

People who can't be chased – because they never ran in the first place.

Acknowledgements

I would like to thank all who made this book possible, especially those who allowed me to interview them for their chapters. These interviews meant I had to ask about some very personal, traumatic and life-changing experiences. I hope I was able to do so with empathy, understanding and compassion. Each of their stories has left a profound and lasting impact on me.

I also want to thank Eilidh MacLennan, Jennie Renton and Gavin MacDougall at Luath Press for all their support.

A huge thanks to my sister Anna and her husband Jim for their proofreading talents, John and Sharron for their support over many years and my mum for everything she has done throughout my life.

Finally, lots of love to my wife Fiona and daughter Chloe for all their support and encouragement.

Luath Press Limited

committed to publishing well written books worth reading

LUATH PRESS takes its name from Robert Burns, whose little collie Luath (*Gael.*, swift or nimble) tripped up Jean Armour at a wedding and gave him the chance to speak to the woman who was to be his wife and the abiding love of his life. Burns called one of the 'Twa Dogs' Luath after Cuchullin's hunting dog in Ossian's *Fingal*. Luath Press was established in 1981 in the heart of Burns country, and is now based a few steps up the road from Burns' first lodgings on Edinburgh's Royal Mile. Luath offers you distinctive writing with a hint of unexpected pleasures.

Most bookshops in the UK, the US, Canada, Australia, New Zealand and parts of Europe, either carry our books in stock or can order them for you. To order direct from us, please send a £sterling cheque, postal order, international money order or your credit card details (number, address of cardholder and expiry date) to us at the address below. Please add post and packing as follows: UK – £1.00 per delivery address; overseas surface mail – £2.50 per delivery address; overseas airmail – £3.50 for the first book to each delivery address, plus £1.00 for each additional book by airmail to the same address. If your order is a gift, we will happily enclose your card or message at no extra charge.

Luath Press Limited
543/2 Castlehill
The Royal Mile
Edinburgh EH1 2ND
Scotland
Telephone: +44 (0)131 225 4326 (24 hours)
Email: sales@luath.co.uk
Website: www.luath.co.uk